"I could never have aspired to four gold medals and a life of achievement without using the law of attraction. I love this book: it is a must read for anyone who wants to create the life he or she wants." —**Tony Volpentest, 4-Time Gold Medalist, and author of** *Fastest Man in the World*

"*Electric Living* is the real deal when it comes to the Law of Attraction. Kolie's philosophy of Consciousness Creates is the key that unlocks the door to tremendous wealth. This book is a must-read for anyone who wants to be successful in life." —**Freeway Ricky Ross**

"Kolie Crutcher has written a truly phenomenal work! I'm a firm believer in the Law of Attraction, and Kolie is like a young Bob Proctor. *Electric Living* is a required reading for all of my students." —**Derek Fonseca, Owner, South Beach Enterprises**

"In this very intriguing book, Kolie shares the science behind the law of attraction and the art of making it work in your life, so that you actualize your dreams and goals!" —**Charmaine Hammond, best-selling author of** *On Toby's Terms,* **and,** *GPS Your Best Life—Charting Your Destination and Getting There in Style*

"In this wonderfully heady book, the founder of *GET MONEY Magazine*, Kolie Crutcher, explains a concept that can change your life. I know, because my life was more or less that of a typical young adult filled with the frustrations of how to sort out opportunities, setbacks, and roadblocks. All challenging were the varied assortment of all relationships—from my parents to teachers to friends, and girlfriends, everyone making demands, leaving me to wonder if I owned any time of my own. But then I discovered the Law of Attraction, studied it—Kolie being one of my mentors—and put into place the principles. It worked, and my life changed for the better—and I do mean better. I was so convinced, I even wrote a book, called *The Law of Attraction for Teens: How to Get More of the Good Stuff and Get Rid of the Bad Stuff*, because I knew how powerful this basic but potent universal law could be for teens in helping them feel more in charge of their lives. Kolie gets my thumbs up on this amazing book, one that can put you on the path for living a bigger, brighter and better life. **—Christopher Combates, author of *The Law of Attraction for Teens: How to Get More of the Good Stuff and Get Rid of the Bad Stuff***

"Kolie Crutcher's *Electric Living* is a brilliant work. Kolie succeeded not only in looking at the Law of Attraction from a purely scientific point of view, but also in delivering a highly complex subject matter in a format that makes it really exciting to read. *Electric Living* provides unique insights into how to positively influence your daily life. This is a truly inspiring book!" **—Pascal Niedermann, CEO, The Maestro Group, New York**

KOLIE CRUTCHER

BETTIE YOUNGS BOOKS

About the Cover:
The inspiration behind the *Electric Living* cover is that electricity is not merely a part of our lives; it literally is life. Human beings are electromagnetic fields (which attract) whose frequency and strength vary with thinking (light bulb). The glowing light bulb represents our consciousness being "on," allowing us the see the abundant beauty in life, and to see that the Law of Attraction operates because we are literally electricity and the fundamental property of electricity is attraction.

Cover Design by Luis Llanos
Text Design by Jane Hagaman
Senior Editor: Elisabeth Rinaldi
Proof Reader: Jazmin Gomez
Author photo by Ron Warner
Publisher: Bettie Youngs Book Publishers

Bettie Youngs Books are distributed worldwide. If you are unable to order this book from your local bookseller or online or from Espresso, you may order directly from the publisher.
BETTIE YOUNGS BOOK PUBLISHERS
www.BettieYoungsBooks.com
info@BettieYoungsBooks.com

ISBN: 978-1-936332-58-8
ePub: 978-1-9363332-59-5

Library of Congress Control Number: 2012913297

1. Crutcher, Kolie. 2. Law of Attraction. 3. Consciousness. 4. Metaphysics. 5. Money. 6. Self-image. 7. Faith. 8. Goals. 9. Higher Power. 10. Relationships. 11. Self-Help.

Printed in the United States of America

Consciousness Creates

As a man who has devoted his whole life to the most clear-headed science, to the study of matter, I can tell you as a result of my research about atoms this much: There is no matter as such. All matter originates and exists only by virtue of a force which brings the particle of an atom to vibration and holds this minute solar system of the atom together. We must assume behind this force the existence of a conscious and intelligent mind. This mind is the matrix of all matter.
—**Max Planck (Nobel Prize-winning German physicist)**

In other words: *consciousness creates.*

Contents

Acknowledgments... ix

Introduction xi

How to Read Electric Living..xvii

Part I—Understanding

Chapter 1...3
Quantum Physics 101—Consciousness Creates

Chapter 2...11
E=mc2—Everything Is Energy

Chapter 3
The Brain, Heart, and Human Consciousness—Masters of the Universe

Chapter 4...29
The Subconscious Mind—The Partnership between Man and God

Part II—Application

Chapter 5...41
Precision of Decision—Know Exactly What You Want

Chapter 6...51
The Power of the Will—The Chief Aim of Mankind

Chapter 7...61
Becoming a Money Magnet—Getting Hooked On Your Passion

Chapter 8 69
    Action—The First Cause of Emotion

Chapter 9 83
    The Genius Pyramid—Sexed-Up Thinking

Chapter 10 89
    The Sixth Sense—Value Consciousness

About the Author 97
Other Books by Bettie Youngs Book Publishers 99

Acknowledgements

To God for giving me the understanding to write this book—thank you.

Thank you mom and dad for love, support and guidance. Thank you to my beautiful sisters and grandmother for always being there. Thanks to my staff and supporters at *GET MONEY Magazine,* and to Rick and everyone at Freeway Enterprise for dedication and persistence.

To everyone at Bettie Youngs Books, my publisher, a very special thanks for your role in making this book a reality. Thank you, the reader, for choosing my book.

And in the most unique way, thank you to my special friend for the words *"I'm proud of you,"* because sometimes the inspirer needs to be inspired.

Introduction

Electric Living is probably not the first motivational, personal development, self-help book you've read. As a matter of fact, there are hundreds of great inspirational books and audio recordings on how to create and live the life of your dreams. I've read many of them.

Some of the classic and most well-known books are:

Think and Grow Rich by Napoleon Hill
The Magic of Thinking Big by David Schwartz
The Power of Positive Thinking by Norman Vincent Peale
As A Man Thinketh by James Allen
The Richest Man in Babylon by George Clason
The Alchemist by Paulo Coelho
The Science of Getting Rich by Wallace D. Wattles
The Magic of Believing by Claude Bristol

The central theme of the motivational or self-help book is the idea that the reader can somehow change physical objects and conditions in his or her life. Ideally a change in *thinking* means improvement. In other words, by thinking positively, your life will turn out to be positive (you get what you want). Conversely, by thinking negatively, your life will turn out to be negative (you get what you *don't* want). This idea is commonly referred to as The Law of Attraction.

Now, even before the modern age of self-help books as we

know them today, philosophers and thinkers have been pondering the results people got in their lives. Some people were rich, others were poor. Some people were happy, others were unhappy. Some people seemed to have "good luck"; others seemed to have "bad luck." The commonality that separated people from successful and unsuccessful seemed to be the successful persons' fixation on a worthy goal which they were consciously aware of and upon which they constantly *thought*. The unsuccessful person—with his lack of a worthy goal—had nothing worthy to think about. In other words, throughout thousands of years of recorded history and untold numbers of scholars and philosophers, there appeared to be a universal truth that never failed: a person will always attract and become what he or she thinks about and focuses on. In other words, there are two little words which sum up the "success" or "failure" of any human: consciousness creates.

Now, this all sounds simple enough. *Consciousness creates.* So why is it that with all the brilliance and technological advancement, with all the various self-help books, CDs, and the like, so many people remain unhappy and financially unsuccessful? I mean seriously, repeat the phrase "consciousness creates."

Most people have heard of *The Secret*—book and movie— recently made popular internationally by Rhonda Byrne. *The Secret* was based on the idea that so few people knew about this magnificently powerful Law of Attraction. This law can bring a person anything they desire. *The Secret* basically popularized The Law of Attraction into mainstream society so that everybody knew about it. Honestly, if you are into the personal development genre, you would have had to be living under a rock not to have heard of The Secret.

Because of its popularity, it would—at first glance—appear that "the secret" was no longer a secret. It had been given national press coverage and publicity in all of the major media outlets. And since everyone now supposedly knew about the secret and knew about the Law of Attraction, everyone should now be happy millionaires living the lives of their dreams, right?

However, this was not the case. It seemed that "the secret" remained a secret, and I wondered why.

I first heard about the secret when I was an undergraduate at Mississippi State University studying electrical engineering. Someone introduced me to a book called *Think and Grow Rich* by Napoleon Hill. I read it, and something about it captured me. So I read it again. And then I read it again . . . and again. I couldn't stop reading it. To this day, I've probably read *Think and Grow Rich* at least thirty times. My habit is to read some of it every day. I've highlighted it, written endless notes in it, and dissected it to the point that my original copy is falling apart.

Now, maybe because I'm an electrical engineer, I began to think about "the secret" from a scientific point of view. When this idea about some great mystical Law of Attraction—that we can attract things into our life by *thinking* about them— was brought to my attention, I thought about it too from a scientific view.

The word *science* comes from the Latin *scientia*, meaning "knowledge." Knowledge develops from interest. Deeper knowledge leads to understanding. And deeper understanding leads to belief.

The more I began to know about the Law of Attraction, the more I wanted to know. As an engineer, I understood that there was an underlying cause for every effect. As a matter of fact, the core of an engineer's study revolves around understanding physical forces and laws which govern the universe. We harness the forces and laws for the betterment of mankind.

An engineer must understand the laws of his field in order to design beneficial systems and devices.

For example, today we have cool devices such as the iPhone and iPad because engineers understand the laws of electricity (among other scientific laws) to an extent that they can design a device (the iPhone and iPad) to manipulate and take advantage of the laws of electricity. This technology provides us some of the many benefits of electricity instead of giving us the harmful effects (such as being electrocuted as you plug in your iPhone to charge its battery). Because a law—by definition—never deviates, we cannot change a law to give us the results we want. Instead we must change *ourselves* and/or design devices that work *with* the law in a manner that we get the desired outcome.

That's how I began looking at the Law of Attraction. I didn't just want to know about it, I wanted to understand how it operated. I wanted to design a device that would allow a reader to take advantage of the Law of Attraction—for his or her betterment (attainment of desires), instead of detriment (misery and failure).

Similar to the law of gravity, the Law of Attraction is *always* in operation. It is not something that a person "turns on" and "turns off." Therefore, in order for a person to benefit from the Law of Attraction, he must position himself correctly. Here is where the word *understanding* began to take on a whole new meaning: the secret remained a secret because people did not understand how the Law of Attraction operated, not because it was never told to them.

Consciousness creates. Deeply understand this great universal truth, and you will have the key that unlocks the secret.

To help in this process of understanding, I wrote this book. Not just for you, but for myself as well.

Before we begin, you may ask, "What *is* Electric Living?"

Electric Living is a *lifestyle*. It is the lifestyle where you are constantly in position—through understanding—to allow the Law of Attraction to benefit your life *in any way you desire.*

How to Read
Electric Living

Electric Living will position you to benefit from the Law of Attraction. As such, this book is written in two parts: Understanding and Application

Understanding

The first part of *Electric Living* explains the pure science behind the Law of Attraction. The purpose is for you to gain an understanding of the Law. As you read, please keep in mind that the Law of Attraction is just that—a law. It is *always* in operation. There is nothing you can do to change or alter a law. However, it is imperative that you do *understand* the Law because it only through the process of understanding that you are able to position yourself to allow the Law to work for your *benefit*. If you don't understand the law, it will still operate; however, it will most likely work to your detriment. Understanding is a process. It is a relationship that develops between the knower and the object of understanding. This relationship implies the knower has abilities and dispositions with respect to the object of knowledge sufficient to support intelligent behavior. Remember: you cannot change the Law, you can only understand it so that you may begin to place yourself in position to benefit from it.

Application

The second part of this book is about keeping yourself in position to benefit from the Law, by controlling and directing your consciousness. This is the intelligent behavior that results from gaining understanding.

How Electric Living Works

There are four fundamental principles of Electric Living:

1. consciousness creates
2. everything is *energy*
3. *infinite intelligence* is all-powerful, yet humans have free will
4. *subconscious mind* is the blending of the first and third principle

To help in the process of understanding, some terms that will be used throughout this book are defined below:

- **The Law of Attraction (aka The Secret):** Mental/physical law that states that a human being will attract objects, people, and circumstances into his life by thinking about those things.

- **Consciousness (aka Human Consciousness):** A state of being (aware), especially of something within oneself, characterized by sensation, emotion, volition, and thought.

- **Thinking:** Intelligently directed and controlled consciousness. It is comprised of two parts: the Thought is the "what" part generated by the brain, and the Emotion is the "feeling" part generated by the heart.

- **Brain:** Physical organ inside the human body that generates the "what" or the Thought part of Thinking. This "what" has a corresponding electromagnetic field (EMF) that can be measured.

- **Heart:** Physical organ inside the human body that generates the "feeling" or the Emotion part of Thinking. This feeling has a corresponding electromagnetic field (EMF) that can be measured.

- **Subconscious Mind (aka Mind, Thinking Heart):** The blending of the power of Infinite Intelligence with human consciousness. The subconscious mind is *not* a physical organ like the brain or the heart. The subconscious mind does *not* generate its own Thinking (Thought and Emotion), but rather it becomes influenced by and indirectly controlled by repetition of the consistent and dominant Thinking that is generated by the human brain and heart. The Law of Attraction operates through humankind's subconscious mind. It is through the subconscious mind that the power of Infinite Intelligence is guided and directed by human Thinking.

- **Infinite Intelligence (aka Infinite Power):** The all-powerful, infiniteness of all knowledge to be known.

- **Energy:** Everything is energy vibrating at varying frequencies. All of the seemingly different things in our universe are simply different combinations and presentations of the same energy being acted upon and brought into form. All things that exist, exist in their form and position because a force has acted upon them, moving them into those specific forms and positions. As you read, you will naturally begin to think about the objects and conditions you want to bring into your life using the Law of Attraction. Any object or condition you desire is simply energy. Think of them as such.

- **Force:** An influence that causes change.

- **Law:** Corresponds to a force, and implies that the force is always in operation.

- **Understanding:** A relationship between the knower and the object of understanding. This relationship implies that the knower has abilities and dispositions with respect to the object of knowledge sufficient to support intelligent behavior.

The Secret Map

I love this tale of a young man who was seeking treasure. He had heard of a wise old man who lived many regions away, and lore said the old man held a secret map that would unerringly guide its possessor to riches beyond his wildest dreams—if he passed the test. The young man was ambitious, so he decided to seek out the wise old man, pass the test, and get the secret map to riches.

The young man set out on the long journey to the far away region. The region was several days' travel away, but this didn't bother the young man. All he could think of was the riches he was about to possess. As he traveled and neared the region of the wise old man, he gave some thought to what the test could be. Was it a physical test? Would he have to solve a riddle? Would he have to bring the old man a gift? At any rate, he was sure he would pass the test; besides, his fortune was almost within grasp!

As he entered the region where the old man was rumored to live, the young man entered a small hut filled with beautiful artifacts from across the world. It was a glorious collection. Just as he reached out to touch one of the golden artifacts, he heard a voice.

"May I help you?" the voice asked.

"Yes. I'm looking for the wise old man who has the secret map to riches," replied the young man.

"You mean this?" replied the old man. He pulled from his cloak a scroll wrapped in a red ribbon. The boy was ecstatic as he laid his eyes on the map.

"Yes!" He replied.

"I have given the map to many," said the wise old man. "Is that all you want?"

"Yes," replied the boy. "And I'll be on my way."

"Are you sure?"

"Yes. That will be all," replied the boy.

"Very well," replied the wise old man. "I will give it to you—but only on one condition. You must promise to wait until you return to your home village to read this map."

"No problem!" the young man replied. "This map *is* the map to the riches, right?"

"Yes," replied the old man. "This map shows the path to riches."

"Great. So, I'll be on my way now."

"Very well then," replied the wise man.

The young man left the region and made it back to his village in half the time, as he could not wait to see the map to his riches. As the young man unrolled the scroll, his excitement grew. When he looked at the map he saw that everything was written out in beautiful detail. However, there was a problem. The map was written in a long-lost ancient language, which the young man could not comprehend. He had been given the secret map, but it was of no value to him because he did not understand it.

With all thy getting, *get understanding.*
Proverbs 4:7b

PART I

Understanding

Quantum Physics 101— Consciousness Creates

As a man who has devoted his whole life to the most clear-headed science, to the study of matter, I can tell you as a result of my research about atoms this much: There is no matter as such. All matter originates and exists only by virtue of a force which brings the particle of an atom to vibration and holds this minute solar system of the atom together. We must assume behind this force the existence of a conscious and intelligent mind. This mind is the matrix of all matter.

—Max Planck (Nobel Prize-winning German physicist)

In other words . . . *consciousness creates.*

No seriously, that's it. Show's over. Those two little words—consciousness creates—are all there is to this book. If you understand—I mean really understand—that phrase, you can stop reading right now. But, if you'd like to know more about the full significance of that phrase, let's talk a bit more.

Did you know that you can create and have anything you want by *thinking* about it? Because of a phenomenon known as the Law of Attraction, you can form your life exactly as you desire it to be. You can attain the exact income, net worth, car, house, business, spouse, profession, level of happiness—whatever you desire—by *thinking* about those things! Sounds like magic, right? It sounds so incredible that most people pass through their entire lives giving very little effort to monitoring—much less controlling—their Thinking.

Well, the Law of Attraction is not magic. It's *science*. The problem is that very few people *understand* this science. Very few people understand what it really means to *Think*. Henry Ford once stated, "Thinking is the hardest work there is, which is probably the reason so few engage in it." Henry Ford was right. Very few people engage in really Thinking. The vast majority of us do not understand the Law of Attraction. As a consequence, we do not live the fantastically wonderful lives we are capable of living—Electric Living!

Classical Physics vs. Quantum Physics

The biggest hurdle to understanding the Law of Attraction is the average person's familiarity with the operation of things in the *macroscopic* (visible to the naked eye) physical world. This macroscopic physical world is the world of *classical* physics, which explains matter and energy on a scale familiar to the human experience. It explains why the planets move in the universe as they do. It explains why water flows downhill. It even explains why a jet that weights many tons can soar through the air without falling to earth. Classical physics explains our everyday physical world as we know it.

Classical physics (aka classical mechanics) explains matter and energy at the macroscopic level of the scale familiar to human experience.

So even though most people are not physicists or engineers who would have a deep enough understanding of the classical physics to design a jet, everyone *is* familiar with the basic laws of classical physics by virtue of simply living everyday lives in the physical macroscopic world. Everyone knows that a ball thrown into the air will fall back down to earth. Everyone knows not to step out in front of a speeding train if they want to live. And everyone knows that a jet must be traveling at a certain speed in order to soar through the air. In other words, we don't need an in-depth understanding of classical physics in order to safely make it through this world and have an average life. Classical physics is our familiar comfortable world; we live it each and every day.

However, it is this very familiarity with, and basic knowledge of classical physics that greatly hinders us from understanding the Law of Attraction. Our familiarity with classical physics prevents us from really *living* life with the richness and fulfillment of which we are capable if we understood the Law of Attraction. This familiarity prevents us from Electric Living. So why don't we understand? *We don't understand the Law of Attraction because the Law of Attraction actually operates at the atomic and subatomic level (invisible to the naked eye), which is governed not by our familiar classical physics, but by quantum physics.*

Think of quantum physics as dealing with things on a very very small level; the level of atoms and the even smaller particles which make up the atom. Although we cannot see them with our naked eye, everything in our physical world is actually made up of different combinations of atoms. Those atoms are made up of different combinations of smaller subatomic particles called protons, neutrons, and electrons. Furthermore, there are even smaller subatomic particles such as quarks. Scientists are not quite sure how "small," small can get, but what *is* known is that there is a difference between the way things operate at the atomic and subatomic (quantum physics) level, and the way they operate at the macroscopic (classical physics) level. You see, scientists have discovered that when dealing with things on a very, very small scale, the laws of classical physics no longer apply. Things behave very differently. And here is where quantum physics comes into the picture.

Quantum physics (aka quantum mechanics) is the body of scientific principles that explains the behavior of matter and its interactions with energy on the scale of atoms and subatomic particles.

Our familiarity and comfort with classical physics will not allow us to believe certain things which are contrary to what we see in our everyday macroscopic world. For example, we do not believe that a ball thrown into the air will float without falling because we are familiar with the law of gravity. However, the Law of Attraction operates on the quantum level (a level with which we are not familiar). As a result, it is this same familiarity with classical physics that will not allow us to believe we can change circumstances and conditions in our physical lives by controlling our Thinking. In other words, our familiarity with classical physics and our everyday macroscopic world hinders us in understanding and believing in the Law of Attraction.

So let's begin to understand quantum physics, so we can gain an understanding of the Law of Attraction. Trust me, it's not that difficult.

Ok, yes. Quantum physics can seem difficult at first. As you can imagine, quantum physics has very complicated sets of theories and mathematical equations that we do not have the time or the need to get into at this time. However, if you would like to learn more about quantum physics, there are many great text books and websites that offer more detailed explanations. (I included a site at the end of this chapter.)

For our purposes—to gain an understanding of the Law of Attraction—we don't need to grasp the entirety of quantum physics and all its complexities. But we do need to understand the main difference between the way things behave at the quantum level and the way they behave at the classical level. The main difference is this: the results of experiments (what you get) in quantum physics depends on *the presence of an observer and on how the experiment is observed.*

This is worth repeating. Grasping this idea is an absolute must to understanding the Law of Attraction. The results of experiments (what you get) in quantum physics depends on the presence of an observer and on how the experiment is observed.

Another way to state this is that in the realm of quantum physics, observing something actually influences the physical process that is taking place! The following explains an experiment on the nature of light, and its wave-particle duality in quantum physics.

What Is Light?

Quantum physics proves that light is made up of particles. The mathematics and experiments show that light is made up of tiny particles called "photons." We can imagine this. Quantum physics also proves that light travels in waves. And just as the case is with particles, the mathematics and experiments *also* show that light travels in waves. We can imagine this also. *But which one is it?* Is light a particle, or is light a wave? As physicist Robert Anton Wilson noted in the 1920s: "It looks as if the damn light is waiting to see how we're going to do the experiment and then deciding which way it's going to go."

He went on to say that, "The modified Copenhagen view is light is neither waves nor particles *until we look*, and then it adjusts itself *depending on what we're looking at it with*. An electron is not anywhere until we look. And when we look, the electron decides to be somewhere as long as we're looking. As soon as we stop looking, the electron is everywhere again."

What You See Is What You Get

Equally astounding is the following statement by nuclear physicist Jim Al-Khalili regarding the nature of atoms:

"An atom only appears in a particular place if you *measure* it. In other words, an atom is spread out all over the place, until a conscious observer decides to look at it. So the act of measurement or observation creates the entire universe. In everyday terms what this means is that unless we observe a thing, it has no form—no existence in that place. In other words, quantum physics tells us that *seeing the thing creates the thing*.

Literally, what you see is what you get. Consciousness creates. This is the reason why *writing down your goals* is a good idea.

You see, in quantum physics there exists an ultimate inseparability of the observer from the thing observed. This ultimate inseparability does not factor in when speaking of classical physics. In classical physics, the observer is simply a passive measurer whose observation has no influence whatsoever over what happens as he observes.

Now, when speaking of classical physics, it is known that the observer can influence the outcome by doing something (applying an outside force) to the thing observed, but not simply by the act of observing. In other words, in classical physics, the observer's simple awareness or *consciousness* of what is happening is considered as having no effect whatsoever on what is happening. Human consciousness is not a force in classical physics.

However, in quantum physics, simple awareness or consciousness turns out to be not so simple. Consciousness actually affects the physical outcome of what happens! The results of experiments (what you get) depend on whether or not an observer *does* exist, and *how* the results are observed. In other words, the outcome of events is affected by human awareness. *Human consciousness is a force that affects what is created.* Burn this idea into your mind—it will be constantly reinforced throughout this book. So don't worry too much if it doesn't click right now.

The Conversation between Atoms on the Job

Remember the statement earlier in this chapter: "An atom only appears in a particular place if you measure it. In other words, an atom is spread out all over the place, until a conscious observer decides to look at it. So the act of measurement or observation creates the entire universe."

The following overly simplified example sums up quantum physics:

Atom #1: "Okay, the boss (a human) is looking! Let's form something!"

Atom #2: "But what?"

Atom #1: "Well, he's expecting to see a _____. So let's form that."

Atom #2: "How do you know he expects to see a _____?"

Atom #1 "Because that's what he's expecting to see. That's what he believes he'll see, and we don't want to disappoint."

Atom #2: "Okay. Let's do it. He's the boss."

To sum up this chapter, it will be very helpful to watch the YouTube video titled "Dr Quantum— Double Slit Experiment" (http://www.youtube.com/watch?v=DfPeprQ7oGc). The video makes the basics of quantum physics more easily understood.

At the smallest level, quantum physics is a world of dynamic *possibilities*, where nothing really exists in static form until human consciousness is added. This human consciousness is a force which directs this energy of possibility, molding it into the form that we *expect*. So at the end of the day, the very smallest and most basic building blocks or substance of all that can be, are awaiting our consciousness to change them from possibility into reality.

In order to understand the Law of Attraction, we must understand the First Principle of Electric Living. The First Principle of Electric Living is: consciousness creates.

$E=mc^2$— Everything is Energy

The most we know about matter is that it is almost entirely space. It is as empty as the sky. It is almost as empty as a perfect vacuum, although it usually contains a lot of energy. Thought is the only force.
**—Dr. Willis R. Whitney, in an address
before the American Chemical Society, 1925**

In 1905, Albert Einstein brought forward the world's most famous equation: $E=mc^2$. What this equation says is that energy (E) is equal to mass (m) multiplied by the speed of light (c) squared. On the most basic level, energy and mass are interchangeable; they are different forms of the same thing. Matter has mass. Mass is energy.

In other words, *everything is energy*.

We touched on this idea in chapter 1. Going back to the composition of things, all matter—no matter how complex in appearance, form, and presentation—can be broken down into atoms and smaller subatomic particles. The different types of atoms correspond to the fundamental *elements*. As of 2012, there were 118 known elements, and each of these 118 elements are different because they each are composed of a differing number of protons, neutrons, and electrons—the parts that make up the atom. Take a look at the following diagram of an atom illustrating protons, neutrons, and electrons. Now, look around you. Everything you see is made up of the same atoms, varying only in number of protons, neutrons, and electrons. Therefore, at this atomic and subatomic level, everything—all matter—is made up of the same stuff.

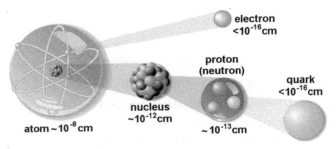

Figure 1. Diagram of an Atom

We identify and distinguish one element from another by *counting the number of protons in the nucleus*. The nucleus of an atom is made up of protons and neutrons. Looking at our example above, if we are to look at the nucleus and say that the darker spheres are neutrons, and the lighter spheres are protons, we will find that the nucleus of this particular atom has thirteen protons. Keep this number in mind as we look at the following table (figure 2), known as the Periodic Table of Elements. This is a simplified version of the table. You've probably seen the full table if you've taken basic chemistry.

You will notice that there are 118 squares (representing the 118 known elements), each with a different number inside. This table is how we organize and distinguish one element from another. Our particular atom shown in figure 1 has thirteen protons in the nucleus. The number of protons in the nucleus is called the *atomic number*. If we look at figure 2, we see that the square with the number 13 also has the letters "Al" in it. This corresponds to the element aluminum. Therefore, we know that an atom with thirteen protons in its nucleus is aluminum.

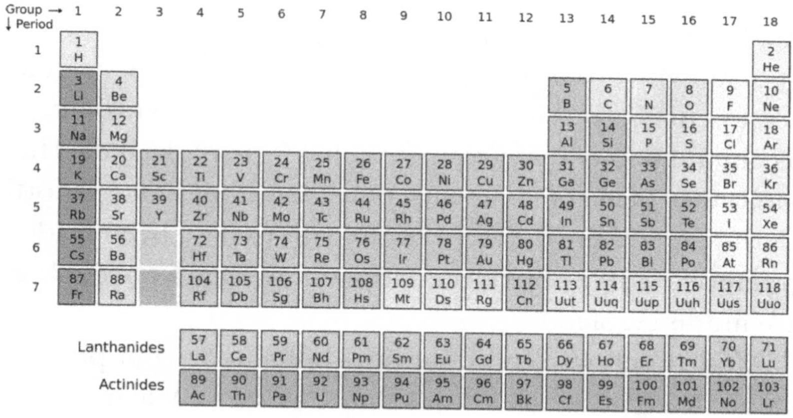

Figure 2. Periodic Table of Elements

Now, here is a key point to keep in mind. If our atom had fourteen protons in the nucleus instead of thirteen, our element would no longer be aluminum (Al). We would then have an atom of silicon (Si). At this quantum level, *one proton* changes the characteristics of a substance from one element to a completely different element!

Again, this is a simplified version of the periodic table.

There are more detailed tables in chemistry books and online which spell out the names of the elements, provide the atomic masses of the elements, and so forth. But for our purposes right now, the important concept to grasp is that everything around you—once you break it down to its most basic parts—is all made up of the same "stuff"—protons, neutrons, and electrons. It is the number of these subatomic particles (specifically protons) in the atom that gives the elements the differing characteristics which separate them.

So Why Do Things Look So Different?

Keep in mind that our eyes cannot detect these extremely small atoms and subatomic particles. Unless we are looking at a substance that is a pure element (such as pure gold), what we see in our macroscopic world is not an element, but a combination of many elements, that form molecules. These molecules may combine with other molecules and so forth. By the time all the different combinations have been made to produce a visible object, the variations of what we actually see are innumerable.

Most things we see in our environment are not pure elements. Even pure water is not a pure element. Water is a molecule—a combination of the pure elements hydrogen (H) and oxygen (O). Water is also a great example of how, when elements are combined, the characteristics of the resulting molecule are often vastly different than the characteristics of either of the elements of which it is comprised.

Now, because water is not an element, we won't see "water" or a symbol for water on the periodic table. Most of us are familiar with water by the name "H_2O". This is the chemical name for water. It literally means that in order to make one part of water, we must take two hydrogen atoms (H_2) and join them with one oxygen atom (O). So if we were to take a spoonful of water, and somehow keep dividing it up, the smallest "piece of water" that we could have (that still has the properties of water) would be represented as in the following figure:

Water molecule

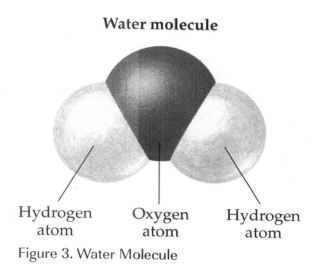

Hydrogen atom   Oxygen atom   Hydrogen atom

Figure 3. Water Molecule

So how is an atom of hydrogen different from an atom of oxygen? Well, if we go back to the periodic table and look at hydrogen (H), we will notice that there is a number 1 in the H box. Oxygen (O) has the number 8 in its box. Remember that each element is different and unique because each is made up of a differing number of protons. Well, a hydrogen atom has one proton. An oxygen atom has eight protons. And that's the difference.

Everything is comprised of the same stuff.

A closer look at each hydrogen and oxygen atom would show the following:

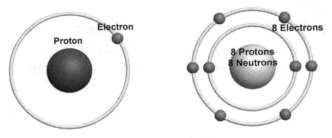

Figure 4. Hydrogen and Oxygen Atoms

For the same reason, you will not see "sugar" listed on the periodic table. However, the molecular symbol for sugar is $C_{12}H_{22}O_{11}$. A sugar molecule has 12 carbon atoms (and according to the periodic table, each carbon atom has 6 protons, 6 neutrons and 6 electrons), 22 hydrogen atoms (each hydrogen atom has 1 proton and 1 electron) and 11 oxygen atoms (each oxygen atom has 8 protons, 8 neutrons and 8 electrons).

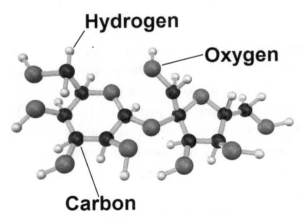

Figure 5. Sugar Molecule

What we begin to see is that the *apparently* large differences (on the macroscopic level) between aluminum, silicon, water, and sugar are only a difference in number and arrangement of protons, neutrons, and electrons at the quantum level.

I use these examples because they are simple, yet they get the point across: all matter is the same, in that it can be broken down to its fundamental elements. These fundamental elements break down into smaller protons, neutrons, and electrons, which break down into smaller particles. The further we break matter down, the more common it becomes. And because of the equation $E=mc^2$, all matter eventually breaks down to be *energy*.

From this point on, we will no longer think of the objects around us as things, but as energy.

That mansion you want is not bricks, wood, and tile. It is protons, neutrons, and electrons. It's energy.

That exotic car you want is not steel, rubber, and carbon fiber. It is protons, neutrons, and electrons. It's energy.

That spouse you want is not skin, teeth, hair, and body. It is protons, neutrons, and electrons. It's energy.

That money you want is not ink and paper. It is protons, neutrons, and electrons. It's energy.

And you, yourself—yep, you're energy, too!

Everything is energy.

If you only take one thing away from this chapter, let it be the habit of viewing all objects in your environment as energy instead of viewing them as solid immutable and unrelated objects. Viewing the objects around you as energy gives you a more intuitive feel of how the Law of Attraction operates.

The Law of Attraction operates at the quantum level. It is operating on all the same energy. Therefore, you need not limit yourself by feeling that a certain thing which you desire is beyond your grasp or "too big to have." Many people limit themselves in this manner. However, when we begin to see that everything is really made of the same stuff, then what's the difference between sugar and aluminum? What's the difference between $100 and $1,000,000,000?

As we end this chapter, take a look at the YouTube video titled "The Detailed Universe" (www.youtube.com/watch?v=_IVqMXPFYwI) posted by PureEducation. This really will blow your mind!

We tend to use our minds for little things instead of big things because we do not understand that all things are just different presentations of the same thing—energy. Let me repeat that. *All things are just different presentations of the same thing—energy.*

In order to understand the Law of Attraction, we must understand the Second Principle of Electric Living. The Second Principle of Electric Living is: everything is energy.

The Brain, Heart, and Human Consciousness— Masters of the Universe

I think, therefore I am.
                    —René Descartes

In the last chapter, we showed that all things—no matter how complex they appear—can be broken down to their fundamental atoms (elements). And these atoms can be further broken down into protons, neutrons and electrons, which can be broken down into smaller particles, and so on. We find that as we break down any substance, all matter is simply energy (as proved by Einstein's formula $E=mc^2$)

Now, let's continue that line of thinking to where you are right now. Look around you and imagine all the things around you—the table, the door, the computer, the water, this book— being broken down and dissolved into smaller and smaller pieces. All these pieces of things would eventually break down into molecules, which would further break down into atoms, which would further break down into protons, neutrons and electrons, then to quarks, and eventually there would simply be the one uniform thing—energy. I like the term "energy of possibility."

Another way to think about this breaking down process is to imagine making a smoothie. To make a smoothie, you may take strawberries, apples, bananas, pineapples, oranges, and milk, and place them into a blender. When you blend everything together, the distinction between all the fruits becomes irrelevant; everything is broken down into a single liquid form whose pieces are so small and uniform that it can be easily consumed through a straw. The different colors, shapes, textures, and characteristics of the fruits are now one and the same. In other words, what was apparently a bunch of different fruits actually turned out to be all the same stuff—the finished smoothie.

Now, looking at this smoothie, what if we wanted to change it back into strawberries, apples, bananas, pineapples, oranges, and milk? Now, you probably don't know how to rearrange the smoothie back into the original fruits, but what is obvious is that *something*—some force—is necessary to rearrange the smoothie back into the form of the original fruits. And behind this force must be a conscious intelligence to ensure that when the one uniform substance or energy of possibility (the smoothie) is rearranged back into the many different forms (the fruits), some of it takes on the form of the bananas, some takes on the form of strawberries, some takes on the form of apples, and so on. If there were no conscious intellect involved in the reforming process, how would things (energy) reorganize?

Therefore, it stands to reason that the fruits—before they were blended—were *also* being held together in their various forms and presentation of seemingly different fruits by some conscious intelligence and force, ensuring that some "stuff" took on the form of a strawberry and some took on the form of an apple, and so forth.

So it is with everything in your environment right now. Because everything is really made up of the one thing—energy—in order for the energy to take on seemingly different forms and representations, a conscious intelligence and a force must be present to arrange the formless energy so that some of the energy arranges and takes on the form of a "door." Some arranges and takes on the form of "water." Some arranges and takes on the form of a "computer." In the absence of this conscious intelligence and force directing the formless energy into specific forms and seemingly different arrangements and positions, the entirety of everything would be only a huge "smoothie" of energy.

The next logical question would be "So why does some energy organize and arrange to take on the form of a "_____" and some energy organizes and arranges to take on the form of a seemingly different "_____"?

If a Tree Falls in the Forest . . .

Many have heard of the age old question, "If a tree falls in the forest, and no one is there to hear it, does it make a sound?" This question stumps a lot of people because they figure that a tree falling always makes a sound. However, the correct answer is, "No, it doesn't make a sound." For the reason that *in the absence of a conscious observer, no sound can exist.*

In chapter 1, we stated that *consciousness creates.* So what exactly is consciousness anyway? According to Merriam-Webster, consciousness is "a state of being (aware), especially of something within oneself, characterized by sensation, emotion, volition, and thought."

It is consciousness that determines why some energy organizes and arranges to take on the form of a "_____" and some energy organizes and arranges to take on the form of a seemingly different "_____." Right now, let's not focus on attracting new things into our lives using the Law of Attraction. Look around you. What's there? What's there right now? Well, if you're reading this, then the most obvious answer is "the book *Electric Living*."

But how do you *know*? Is the book still there if you close your eyes? Try it. Is the book *Electric Living* still there? You will probably reach out and touch the book, and say, "Yes, the book is still there." But what if you had to place your hands behind your back? Now I ask, "Is the book *Electric Living* still there?" You may bring your nose close to the table to try to smell the paper. "Yes, the book is still there." Take away sense of smell. You may try to taste the book. You may ask me to drop it on the table so you can hear the book fall. Finally, if you couldn't see, feel, smell, touch, or hear *Electric Living*, and I asked, "Is the book *Electric Living* still there?" You would have to answer, "I don't know."

What if I switched books, and replaced *Electric Living* with a different book while your eyes were closed? How do you know the book in front of you is *Electric Living*?

You get the idea. My point is that *nothing exists unless we see it*. And by see, I mean sense or observe it. In other words, the only way a thing exists to us is if we are conscious of it. We must detect and measure it's presence by means of one of— or a combination of—our five senses. This is backed up by experiments in quantum physics. Remember the statement from quantum physics: "An atom only appears in a particular place if you measure it. In other words, an atom is spread out all over the place, until a conscious observer decides to look at it. So the act of measurement or observation creates the entire universe."

Remember also from quantum physics that what you get is affected by *how* you are measuring it. As humans, our measuring devices are our five senses. Can you see the color red with your tongue? No. Can you taste an apple by placing it next to your ear? No. You cannot.

Passive versus Active Consciousness

Most people view their consciousness as simply a means— an instrument—to measure and observe their environment and what happens in their physical world. They do not feel that they have any power or control over what happens. They simply observe, react, and get along the best they can, trying to make it through life without too much discredit.

However, this is not the true purpose of human consciousness. It is only the very tip of the iceberg. Yes, the human consciousness is an instrument to observe and measure the outer world; however quantum physics tells us that *it is the very act of observing and measuring the environment that creates the environment.* In other words, as you go along in your day-to-day activities, you are inclined to think that you are simply passively observing something that has already been created. However, the truth is that you are really actively creating *as you observe.*

This simple change in the way you view the world is enormously powerful—if you can understand its significance. View your consciousness as active, not passive. There is no time. Time is humankind's perception of the "space" that lies between a cause and its resulting effect. Everything is created in the now, by observing it.

If an object exists in the here and now only because we are conscious of it, an object can exist in the future only because we are conscious of it. Remember, present objects and circumstances are energy being held in that particular present form and presentation *because there is a consciousness on them.* Take the consciousness away, and they will cease to exist! The energy may form another object or circumstance that fits the mold of the new consciousness because consciousness carries with it an expectation. We call this expectation *belief.*

What to Do When the "Bad Stuff" Happens?

Stop observing it. Don't look at it, hear it, taste it, feel it, smell it, think of it, or otherwise imagine it. *It cannot survive without your consciousness.* Think instead upon your inspiring major purpose or goal in life.

I can't (and won't) begin to talk about all the clutter and confusion people were throwing my way during the process of writing this book. However, I knew the only thing that was important at the time was finishing this book. So I simply chose to pay them no attention. Remember, *consciousness creates.* How you choose to observe the energy around you determines what is ultimately created. The ancient Greek philosopher Epictetus stated, "People are disturbed not by things, but the view they take of them."

Understand this: people want your attention. And whether they realize it or not, people will do anything to get your attention. Attention is the greatest form of currency (that's why it's called "paying" attention). When you place your attention on something, you are placing your consciousness onto it, and you are creating it.

H to the Izzo

One of the most successful rappers and businessmen of our day is Shawn Corey Carter, aka Jay-Z. People rap his lyrics and hum his music all the time without giving the slightest thought to the message that may be encoded in it. As a matter of fact, one of the most catchy songs and chants by Jay-Z is called "Izzo (H.O.V.A)," often referred to as "H to the Izzo," and there is a specific line that stands out to me in that song. It is the following:

"He who does not feel me is not real to me. Therefore he doesn't exist."

Now, I didn't speak with Jay-Z to get his interpretation of this line, but to me, it means the following: if you do not have positive Thinking toward me, I choose to pay no attention to you. And because I choose to pay you no attention, as far as I'm concerned, you don't exist.

Consciousness creates.

Here now, we have an opportunity to redefine the term "thinking." Thinking is intelligently directed and controlled human consciousness. It is comprised of two parts:

1. The Thought is the "what" part generated by the brain.

2. The Emotion is the "feeling" part generated by the heart.

The Brain and Heart

The brain generates the Thought, or the "what" part of Thinking. It helps to picture the Thought as the pure subject matter of Thinking. Because the brain is a physical organ, we can actually measure brain activity of Thought by means of an instrument called an Electroencephalogram (EEG). Alpha, beta, theta, delta, and gamma waves are different types of waves produced by the brain. Each of these common types of waves (along with other, less common waves), has a characteristic amplitude and frequency. This amplitude and frequency corresponds to specific types of Thoughts. For instance, alpha waves are produced when sitting in a relaxed position with eyes closed. Beta waves (the most common type of waves) are produced during times of concentrated mental activity. Delta waves are found during times of deep sleep. The point is that each of these waves has a characteristic electrical amplitude and frequency which varies according to the specific Thought of the brain at that time. *Thought is electrical activity. This electrical activity produces an electromagnetic field (EMF).*

The heart generates the "feeling" or the Emotion part of Thinking. The Emotion gives color and vibrancy to the Thought. In the same fashion that an EEG measures the electrical activity of the brain, an electrocardiogram (ECG or EKG) measures the electrical activity of the heart. *Emotion is electrical activity. This electrical activity produces an electromagnetic field (EMF).* The heart is much more than a pumping station for the body's blood. The electromagnetic field radiated by the heart permeates every cell of the body. The heart's electromagnetic signal is so strong that it radiates a 360-degree sphere all around you, and as far as ten feet into the area outside of your skin. The heart produces by far the body's strongest electromagnetic fields.

In laboratory experiments, electromagnetic fields have been shown to affect atoms. Coincidentally, we know from quantum physics that human consciousness affects atoms as well.

For our purposes, it is easy to picture the brain as generating the Thought, and the heart producing the Emotion. In reality, both the Thought of the brain and the Emotion of the heart affect each other and blend into what we know as consciousness. And both are ultimately controlled by the actions of the person (more on this in chapter 8). This consciousness—in the most simple of terms—can be pictured as an electromagnetic field produced by the brain combined with an electromagnetic field produced by the heart. Electromagnetic fields affect atoms. *Consciousness creates.*

Remember from chapter 2 that everything is energy. Well, it turns out that this energy is electromagnetic radiation. And electromagnetic radiation is a particular form of the more general electromagnetic field. This is the same electromagnetic field that is produced by the human brain and heart.

In essence, the electromagnetic fields generated by the brain and the heart, as a person has a Thought or an Emotion, are the same energy that forms the basis of all matter.

The Subconscious Mind—
The Partnership between
Man and God

For as he thinketh in his heart, so is he.
—Proverbs 23:7a

Throughout the ages, humans have been aware of an infinite source of knowledge and intelligence that powers all. This infinite source gives us life, automatically providing us a heartbeat and breath—even as we sleep. This same infinite source also powers the Law of Attraction. Depending on the culture or religion, many refer to this infinite source as "Infinite Intelligence" or "God."

Bill Gates once said, "Information is the reduction of uncertainty." Theoretically, if one knows *everything*, then there is nothing that he or she cannot do. And so it is that as humans we feel limited and less powerful when we don't know—when we lack information. When humanity lacks information, we turn to the source—God.

Now, by all accounts, God has unlimited power because

he is the storehouse of all that exists to be known. There is no uncertainty when speaking of God. There is nothing he *can't* do. Continuing along this line of thinking, this means that God *could* change the laws of nature if he wanted to (the phrase "if he wanted to" implies being conscious). Also, he *could* change the Law of Attraction if he wanted to. But also by definition, a law *never* changes. As a matter of fact, God never changes. That's the reason we have faith in God and in the Law. *They never change,* and there is no possibility of them ever changing. Quite honestly, if the Law of Attraction *could* change, there is really no reason for reading this book. This book is about a *law* that operates 100 percent (not 99.999 percent) of the time, *with no possibility of deviation.* The moment a law has a possibility of deviating, it ceases to be a law. Therefore, even God himself could not change it. But wait a minute. This places a boundary on God's unlimited power. This poses a contradiction. How can God's unlimited power remain unlimited, while at the same time, allowing no possibility of a law deviating—even if that deviation were to be caused by God?

Here's how to solve this contradiction. *A truly unlimited power must be unconscious.* God, as the storehouse of all the knowledge and power that exists is not aware of his own existence in the same manner that humans are aware of things. The existence of an unconscious God is the only rationale to explain how a law can never have the possibility of deviating, without—at the same time—bounding or placing a restriction on the unlimited power of God. Although consciousness creates, *any consciousness or awareness also acts as a boundary or limitation,* in much the same way that when a spotlight focuses on a certain area, there remains an area outside the spotlight that remains dark. The bottom line is that a truly unlimited power must be *un*conscious. In other words, it has no aware-ness of itself and its power.

And here is where humans, and their consciousness—or awareness—comes into play. The power of God or Infinite Intelligence is known only through human consciousness.

Man Is in Control

Right now I'm sitting inside my Corvette—Yvette. And I've got more than 400 horsepower under my hood. This is a lot of power—way more than I can generate on my own if I were just walking down the street. This is all well and good, but what now? With all of this horsepower I have access to right now, what's going to happen? Well, I'm just sitting here waiting, so all this power really isn't doing anything. I'm not moving. I'm not flying down the freeway doing 180 miles per hour. I'm just sitting here. Great. Why aren't all these horses doing anything? I want to go. Come on, let's go! These horses seem to be asleep. It's like they don't even know they exist! What are they waiting for? Hmmm. Maybe they're waiting on . . . me. Let's push the start button and see what happens? Vvvrrroommm! Ah, there we go!

Okay, so what's my point? The pinnacle of power "awaits" instruction by the conscious Thought of man. Picture an elec-trical outlet in your home or office. The power isn't going to just jump out of the wall and say, "I want to turn on this light, but I don't want to turn on this computer." Even in the midst of the all-powerful Infinite Intelligence, it is man who has the free will to decide his own fate.

In order to understand the Law of Attraction, we must under-stand the Third Principle of Electric Living. The Third Principle of Electric Living is: infinite intelligence is all-powerful, yet man has free will.

This is how life operates. There exists an Infinite Intelligence that knows no boundaries and can do literally anything! Yet, even in situations where Infinite Intelligence seems to act without instruction from man, man is *always* in control (though many times he is *not* controlling intelligently). Most of us tend to view God as acting strictly on his own accord because we are unaware that our consciousness is at all times providing the instruction. Many times, situations and circumstances do not play out as we expect them to play out in the short term. We anticipate things going a certain way. But they do not. So we throw in the towel and say, "Well, God intervened. Maybe this was not meant to be." However, what we must keep in mind is that the *end result* is always up to us, although the intermediate steps and ways and means of getting there are not always clear to us. In other words, God only acts on his "own accord" for the purpose of providing *you* that thing you desire. Humans have free will that is always in operation.

When you are consciously Thinking, what you are doing is giving an instruction. This is an instruction that says what you want. This instruction meets with the power to get it done inside the subconscious mind. Remember that in order for a Thought to mix with power of Infinite Intelligence, the Thought must be mixed with an Emotion. When Infinite Intelligence comes into the subconscious mind, it doesn't "know" what to do. There is no innate motive or desire on the part of Infinite Intelligence—God. What can he do? Everything. What improvement can he make? None. Can he get more money? Can he buy up more real estate in the universe? No. You see, by simply being all there is, relativity disappears and no meaning can exist. *Meaning can only exist as a conscious individual ponders his limits and strives to attain by constantly rede-*

fining those limits. Therefore, in order for God to be happy, *we* must be happy. This is done by means of the limited consciousness of man. As man changes his consciousness, he redefines his limits, which provides meaning and happiness. To know everything is to know nothing. Therefore the cup is always empty. Man's consciousness adds to God's cup.

Tony Robbins wrote a wonderful book titled *Awaken the Giant Within.* I suggest you read it. And the title is perfectly chosen. Awaken the giant within! There is an infinite power within you that's just sitting there, waiting for you to awaken it by telling it exactly what *you* want. You!

Too many times, people wait for God to give them a sign because of some feeling that "God knows everything and I know nothing." I'm sorry, but this is not the way to think. Each of us has access to a power of unlimited magnitude, but it is *us* who must push the start button to awaken it.

Remember, this is a partnership. You provide the conscious Thought, meaning what you want. Exercise your free will. Infinite Intelligence will provide the power to get it done. Now, this is not to say that as the power is being provided you are going to know everything or see everything clearly each step of the way. This is not your concern. Remember, it is not *you* that is the infinite storehouse of knowledge. Decide what you want, emotionalize it, and then Infinite Intelligence will make it happen.

What It Means To Think—Mental Maturity

Imagine a two-year-old sitting in front of a computer. What will happen? Well, more than likely, the child will begin to start randomly hitting keys. There is no telling what will pop up on the monitor. Who knows what program the child will open, what website it will go to, or what will appear on the screen. Believe it or not, this is how most people go blundering through life. People can't understand why all of these crazy, undesirable results keep "popping up" on their life's monitor (their circumstances). What must be clearly understood is that your Thoughts and Emotions are the "hitting of keys" on the computer. They determine what pops up on your life's monitor. Until you can get to the point of controlling your Thought and Emotion, you are mentally immature. You are basically the same as a two-year-old with no control, simply banging away at the keyboard in front of you, the result being all kinds of crazy things popping up on the monitor. Thinking is intelligently directed and controlled consciousness.

Consciousness + Unconsciousness = Subconscious

The Law of Attraction operates because humans—*with their consciousness*—actually guide and direct the unconscious Infinite Power. When we speak of the Law of Attraction, the things we "attract" into our lives come to us because we have blended our consciousness with the unconscious power of Infinite Power. This combination is the subconscious mind. Once Thinking has entered the subconscious mind, the result is the physical manifestation of the Thinking—by any means necessary.

Here's the tricky part about consciousness. It's also the reason why so few people are successful. During the course of an average day, we allow so many things to hit our consciousness. If your willpower is not sufficiently strong, an unwanted Thought can slip past and get into your subconscious mind without you even noticing it. One negative Thought driven by Emotion and fostered by the subconscious mind is enough to destroy all chances of success. The good news is that a Thought in and of itself is not sufficiently strong to make its way into the subconscious mind. The Thought must be repeated many times, and mixed with Emotion.

Remember that our subconscious mind is not a physical organ such as the brain or heart. Rather, the subconscious mind (aka "the mind" or "the thinking heart") is more aptly described as our frequency of Emotion mixed with our dominating Thought. We are really a mind that has a physical body rather than a physical body that has a mind.

As a man *thinketh* in his *heart,* so is he. The subconscious mind is the seat of belief.

What all human beings are attempting to do—whether they know it or not—is impress their conscious Thoughts onto the unlimited power of unconscious Thinking. The result being direction and control of the power that brings the particles of the atom together to form all we know. Consciousness creates.

In the last chapter, we stated that a Thought is an electrical impulse generated by the brain. These electrical impulses take on the form of waves and can be measured by an EEG. Additionally, these electrical impulses will create electrical and magnetic fields. Now, in the same fashion, when we feel, or have an emotion, our hearts generate electrical impulses (measurable by an EKG), which also create electrical and magnetic fields.

Our subconscious mind acts as a safety valve of sorts. It ensures that we do not automatically attract every single Thought that our brains think about. This is important, because we cannot completely control every Thought impulse that enters our brains. Our brains are hardwired to our five senses, and these five senses are constantly bombarded with information. Think about it. If this were the case, a person could show you a picture of a gigantic purple elephant and because you see this picture, and you now have a Thought about it, a gigantic purple elephant appears out of nowhere.

However, once a Thought generated by the brain is combined with the Emotion of the heart, the "attraction" begins! The Law of Attraction actually operates because the Emotion generated by the heart literally drives a Thought (idea, plan, or purpose) into contact with the source of infinite power. A pure Thought has no power unless it rides the wave of Emotion into contact with unconscious Infinite Power. Emotion can be developed by repetition of the Thought. Once a conscious Thought has been introduced to the unconscious Infinite Power (by means of the subconscious mind), the Thought will manifest itself into its physical counterpart by the most expedient manner possible.

From now on, we must understand that Thinking is not just associated with the brain, but with the heart. This is because the Emotional component of Thinking is what allows a Thought from the brain to be driven into the subconscious mind where that Thought is introduced to the Infinite Power to manifest it. To reiterate the significance of the heart when dealing with driving a Thought into the subconscious mind, let's revisit the electromagnetic fields generated by the heart as touched upon in the previous chapter. The human heart generates the strongest electrical fields in the body. The human heart also generates the strongest magnetic fields in the body. Together, these are known as electromagnetic fields (EMF).

Our physical world hinges largely on electrical and magnetic fields. And it just so happens that if you change either the electrical field or the magnetic field of an atom, you will change that atom.

Our hearts generate *both.*

Our hearts generates electrical fields that are 60–100 times stronger than the electrical fields generated by our brains, and magnetic fields 5,000 times stronger than those generated by the brain. The electrical and magnetic fields created by our brains are relatively weak when compared with those created by the heart. This is why world events are shaped more by how people feel as opposed to simply hard reason.

Emotions are severely underestimated in our culture. The human heart does more to cause success than any form of talent, knowledge, or education. Ask any successful person the key to his or her success, and each will say "I do what I love."

Conversely, a common mental blunder is the idea that it is somehow "okay" to constantly express negative emotion because of the actions of another. There can be nothing good that can come from prolonged and constant Emotion of anger, fear, or any of the other negative emotions. This is a law. A person cannot plant an apple seed and get oranges.

Many people live their lives expressing negative Emotions such as jealousy, hatred, anger, envy, and fear because they feel they have some sort of license to feel a certain way and express those negative emotions because of something someone did to them. This type of thinking can only backfire and bring negative results into the life of the person expressing the negative Emotion because *positive results in life cannot come from negative Emotion in the heart.*

All positive Emotions should be expressed because we never know exactly how and when the results will return into our lives. By means of the subconscious mind, a human being and God become one.

In order to understand the Law of Attraction, we must understand the Fourth Principle of Electric Living. The Fourth Principle of Electric Living is: the subconscious mind is the blending of our consciousness with Infinite Intelligence.

PART II

Application

Precision of Decision— Know Exactly What You Want

People with goals succeed because they know where they're going. It's that simple.
—Earl Nightingale

Success. *Know exactly what you want.*

Ninety-five percent of people don't *know* what they want. They don't *know* where they're going. As a result, the vast majority of people sabotage success before they begin on the journey. Knowing exactly what you want and expressing it as a *precisely decided* written goal is the first and most important step in attaining success. In the absence of a precisely defined written goal, the Law of Attraction can only work *against* you, not for your benefit. "I want to be rich," is not a goal. "I want to be famous," is not a goal. These are vague descriptions of conditions that people wish for, yet have no power whatsoever.

Precision of decision is a term I like to use to describe not only the conscious act of making a *decision* on what you want in life, but the process of fine-tuning your decision so that it is as exact and detailed as possible.

Here, it is in order to define both the terms *decision* and *precision*:

- decision—a conscious choice *that you do not waver from*
- precision—exactness

The purpose of this chapter is to show—from a scientific standpoint—why precision of decision positions you to benefit from the Law of Attraction.

Looking at the definitions of *decision* and *precision*, they appear simple enough. But we must understand and internalize what they really mean. For example, when you make a *true* decision, you do not change your mind according to which way the wind blows. You are not influenced to change your mind by the opinions of others. You do not throw in the towel when situations and circumstances in life become difficult. The truest test of a decision is in the ability to stand by that decision in the face of all obstacles and difficulties.

In the same vein, precision means that you detail all aspects of your decision as exactly as possible. Okay, so you want a new house. That's your decision. But how big do you want the house to be? How many square feet? How many bedrooms? How many bathrooms? Do you want an indoor, heated pool? Do you want a Jacuzzi in the bedroom? Do you want a three-car garage? Do you want a chef, a housekeeper, a butler? What color do you want the cabinets in the kitchen? Do you want marble or granite countertops? Do you want dark or light hardwood floors in the living room? How big do you want the entertainment room? You get the idea.

Write all of the details out on paper so you can obsc. them. Print out pictures of exactly what you want. Some people may say that this is a lot of effort. I disagree. It seems fun to me. You have an opportunity to go into endless detail about exactly what you want. We do it as kids at Christmas time, but as adults, we tend to forget about it.

Regardless of whether you view the process of precision of decision as "fun" or as "effort," it works! There is a scientific reason it works. It doesn't work just because Kolie Crutcher says it works. It doesn't work because Napoleon Hill, or Earl Nightingale, or Norman Vincent Peale, or any motivational speaker or writer says it works. It works because *quantum physics* says it works. Remember from chapter 1, that quantum physics tells us that *it is the act of observation that creates.* Consciousness creates.

When you write down a goal on paper, what you have done is really *observe* it for the first time as *yours.* You have officially become *conscious* of it. The act of consciousness is what creates. Consciousness creates. Consciousness creates. I'm going to be repeating this throughout this book because it is so simple, yet millions live their lives in failure and misery simply because they allow themselves to remain conscious of all the things they *don't* want. We must get into the habit of becoming conscious of our desires instead of our fears.

Also, when you practice precision of decision, you don't have to compete with everybody. As a matter of fact, you don't have to compete with anybody. The vast majority of people spend their lives browsing around, "window-shopping" and trying to figure out what they want. Remember that the world is abundant, and deciding what you want gives you the right to have it. No one can take anything from you once you've made the decision to have it. It belongs to you. There is enough energy in the universe so that everyone can have what they want. But we must first make the precise decision on what that will be. Set your consciousness on that which you desire.

It is the act of observation that creates the thing. Consciousness creates.

This is shown by quantum physics. Therefore, it only stands to reason that you cannot create a thing unless you observe the thing and are conscious of the thing. When it comes to getting something you've never had before, you must find ways to become conscious of it in your imagination and do everything in your power to *remain* conscious of it even before you take physical possession of the thing.

There seems to be a magic in precision of decision. I said magic, but it's really not magic. Precision of decision can appear to be magic because people don't understand it. But it's a scientific principle. The word *magic* connotes some type of trick or foolery that people do not trust. But this is not magic. It is simply the way the great universal law known as the Law of Attraction operates, and precision of decision is a habit we must form in order to position ourselves to benefit from that law.

Again, you must understand that you are not "making" the Law of Attraction work, but rather "positioning yourself" so that the Law of Attraction *benefits* you. As such, it is essential to be extremely precise in what you want and in setting goals because *nature and the universe are always precise.* The universe doesn't "change its mind." And because the universe operates so precisely, *you too* must be precise if you want to benefit from the Law of Attraction. In nature, very small, seemingly insignificant differences, determine what "is" and "is not." To understand this, let's look at the periodic table of the elements again.

Alchemy—Turning Lead into Gold

In chapter 2, when we first looked at the periodic table of the elements, we used it to show that all matter (energy)—no matter how complex—is comprised of some combination of the basic elements. Here, we will revisit the table for the purpose of showing the importance of being precise when setting goals and stating what you want in life. There are 118 elements occurring naturally, and about two dozen that have been created through nuclear reactions in research laboratories.

Group → ↓ Period	1	2	3	4	5	6	7	8	9	10	11	12	13	14	15	16	17	18
1	1 H																	2 He
2	3 Li	4 Be											5 B	6 C	7 N	8 O	9 F	10 Ne
3	11 Na	12 Mg											13 Al	14 Si	15 P	16 S	17 Cl	18 Ar
4	19 K	20 Ca	21 Sc	22 Ti	23 V	24 Cr	25 Mn	26 Fe	27 Co	28 Ni	29 Cu	30 Zn	31 Ga	32 Ge	33 As	34 Se	35 Br	36 Kr
5	37 Rb	38 Sr	39 Y	40 Zr	41 Nb	42 Mo	43 Tc	44 Ru	45 Rh	46 Pd	47 Ag	48 Cd	49 In	50 Sn	51 Sb	52 Te	53 I	54 Xe
6	55 Cs	56 Ba		72 Hf	73 Ta	74 W	75 Re	76 Os	77 Ir	78 Pt	79 Au	80 Hg	81 Tl	82 Pb	83 Bi	84 Po	85 At	86 Rn
7	87 Fr	88 Ra		104 Rf	105 Db	106 Sg	107 Bh	108 Hs	109 Mt	110 Ds	111 Rg	112 Cn	113 Uut	114 Uuq	115 Uup	116 Uuh	117 Uus	118 Uuo

Lanthanides	57 La	58 Ce	59 Pr	60 Nd	61 Pm	62 Sm	63 Eu	64 Gd	65 Tb	66 Dy	67 Ho	68 Er	69 Tm	70 Yb	71 Lu
Actinides	89 Ac	90 Th	91 Pa	92 U	93 Np	94 Pu	95 Am	96 Cm	97 Bk	98 Cf	99 Es	100 Fm	101 Md	102 No	103 Lr

Figure 5. Periodic Table of Elements

The table can seem very complex, but I want to draw your attention to the box that contains "Au" and the number 79. Au is the chemical symbol for gold. In chapter 2, we saw that the number 79 represents the atomic number of gold. Now look just to the right: that box contains the symbol "Hg" and the number 80. Hg is the chemical symbol for mercury. Now, which one do you want? Would you rather have an ounce of gold or an ounce of mercury?

Quite naturally, you would choose to have the gold because gold is much more valuable than mercury. As I wrote this, I checked the price of gold on the New York Stock Exchange. It closed at $1,754.38 per ounce yesterday. Mercury (which isn't even traded on the NYSE) is worth around $9.37 per ounce. This is a big difference in trading value. But there are more differences between gold and mercury. For instance, mercury is not even solid at room temperature. It's a liquid. We place a high value on gold for many reasons. But what's the real difference between gold and mercury? For the answer, we need to look closer at the periodic table of elements. Notice that the box labeled "Au" has an atomic number 79 in it. Also notice that the box labeled "Hg" has the atomic number 80 in it. The numbers 79 and 80 represent the atomic number, which is the number of protons in the nucleus. So *at the quantum level, the difference between gold and mercury is 1 proton.*

The same is true if you want to "turn lead into gold" as the alchemists claimed to have the power to do. On a large scale, it may seem like magic to turn lead (which has a comparatively small value) into gold. But, if we look on the periodic table, we will see that lead (Pb), with an atomic number of 82, is only three positions to the right of gold (Au), which has an atomic number of 79. So again, at the quantum level, the difference between lead and gold is only 3 protons. However, on the large scale that we interpret as humans, the difference between lead ($0.05 per ounce) and gold ($1,754.38 per ounce) is large. It is for this reason, that one cannot simply say, "I want a lot of money." The universe does not operate in terms of "a lot." It operates in terms of very precise quantities. What is "a lot" of protons in the nucleus of an atom? Is it 79 protons, or is it 82 protons? Who knows? To the uninformed, 3 little protons may not matter much. But as we can see from the previous example, those 3 little protons at the quantum level—the level at which the Law of Attraction operates—make all the difference between receiving lead and receiving gold. Which do you want? Be precise.

Without getting bogged down in all the complexities of chemistry, know that it is *the atomic number (the number of protons in the nucleus of the atom) alone that determines the chemical properties of an element.*

On a quantum level, the small things make a huge difference. The universe operates in terms of precision. Nothing happens until something is precisely decided upon.

Form the Habit of Precision of Decision

I have a habit of keeping a weekly Excel spreadsheet. This spreadsheet is divided into 168 cells, one cell for each hour of the day for the entire week. I've been keeping this spreadsheet for a while, and it has been a great tool for me. I've found that *when I write something into my spreadsheet, it gets done.*

Do I always get everything done on my spreadsheet at the time I have it planned? No. But the spreadsheet lets me know when I'm off track. And then I can adjust myself to get back on track.

For example, I set a goal to wake up at 5 a.m. each morning. Sometimes I don't wake up until 5:05 or 5:10. Sometimes I don't get up until 6 a.m. Sometimes I wake up at 4 a.m. In a few instances, if I'm traveling or have a deadline to meet, I don't get to bed *until* 5 a.m. The point is that I know my goal each morning is to wake up at 5 a.m., so in the event that I don't wake up on time (the excuse doesn't matter), I know that I must adjust myself the next night so that I *do* wake up at 5 a.m. Maybe I need to eat earlier. Maybe I need to go to sleep in a better mood. Maybe I need to arrange my schedule differently. This is the purpose of goals. *When you set a precisely defined goal, you will—over time—adjust yourself to the form of that goal.* So set big goals! You may not be able to see much difference from one hour to the next, but as more and more days pass, the end result will be astounding. Similarly, the difference (3 protons) between an atom of lead and an atom of gold may not seem significant on the quantum level, but as more and more atoms join and become visible to the naked eye, the difference in the end results will be astounding.

Many people don't set goals because they don't think they can achieve them. Or, having set a goal, and missed it, they become discouraged. Your life is a journey. You are not always going to make the right moves, but you *do* need to know when you are off course. And there is no way to know if you are off course unless you have established a predetermined goal. If you know you missed your exit on the freeway, you can turn around or find another way to get to your destination—*if you know exactly where you are going.* But if you don't even know where you're going, you'll just keep driving to—well, who knows? I guess you'll just drive until you run out of gas.

Think of a decision as being a reflection in the mirror. Making quick decisions is a reflection that you know what you want.

As you read this book, keep in mind that you are attempting to allow a great universal law—a law that is always at work—to benefit you. In that regard, you must position yourself so that you can benefit. The difference between huge success and failure is often times very small, and seemingly insignificant. On an elemental quantum level, the difference between gold and mercury is only 1 proton. The difference between lead and gold is only 3 protons.

If you cannot formulate a precise decisiveness about what

you want, the Law of Attraction cannot operate for your benefit. According to nature, something either is, or it's not. You are now attempting to adjust your consciousness. Because it is consciousness that creates, you must move your consciousness from a mere awareness to Thinking. Thinking is intelligently directed and controlled human consciousness. And the first step to Thinking is precision of decision.

Time Management

All time management problems are actually a lack of precision of decision. Once you have decided what you truly want to do—and I mean truly *decided*—you will find that you no longer have problems managing your time.

Time is the most basic currency. There has never been a second in the history of the universe where the universe was simply sitting back idling, doing nothing and wasting time, while it was trying to figure out what to do with itself. Every millisecond in existence has been utilized in the movement toward something precisely defined. Remember, *time is man's perception of the "space" that lies between a cause and its resulting effect.* Once you—as an individual—get to the point of precisely deciding what it is that you want, you recapture time and the infinite power of the universe begins to move in your favor.

The Power of the Will—
The Chief Aim of Mankind

Just as electricity will turn the wheels of industry, and render useful service if used constructively, or snuff out life if wrongly used, so will the law of autosuggestion lead you to peace and prosperity, or down into the valley of misery, failure, and death, according to your degree of understanding and application of it.

—**Napoleon Hill,** *Think and Grow Rich,* **1937**

I am an electrical engineer. I graduated from Mississippi State University with a bachelor of science degree in electrical engineering. As a result, I have a deep understanding of nature's laws of electricity, and how to apply those laws for the betterment of our world. Electricity is both powerfully constructive and destructive at the same time. And because I am an electrical engineer, I understand how to control and direct electricity so that man is not harmed by, but rather becomes the benefactor of, electricity's unyielding power.

Consciousness too is both powerfully constructive and destructive—*depending on how we use it.* Just as electricity must

51

be controlled and directed by the electrical engineer in order to make constructive use of this power (and avoid destructive consequences of this power), each person must too control and direct his or her consciousness to make constructive use of this power (and avoid destructive consequences of this power). *Consciousness is the first cause, the first force that ultimately causes everything.* My goal in writing this book is to allow you, the reader, to understand this truth. Once you understand this, you will never again play with your consciousness or leave it uncontrolled and undirected.

Understand: you cannot *stop* your consciousness. But you can *control* your Thinking. This ability to control our Thinking is our divine right as humans. It separates us from all other forms of life, and places us at the table with the King of Kings!

In the last chapter, we defined a decision as a conscious choice that you *do not waver from.* To ensure that a decision remains a decision—that you do not waver from in the face of adversity or ridicule—requires power. This power is known as *willpower.*

POME (Product of My Environment)?

As a human—a king or a queen—you are *not* a product of your environment. Your environment is a product of you! Because of the Law of Attraction, your consciousness produces a product, which is your environment. So your environment is actually a product of *you,* not the other way around. So why do so many swear by "I'm a product of my environment?" Well, just because many people buy into a cliché doesn't make it true.

Here's the truth: until you understand how to really control your Thinking, you will *appear* to be a product of your environment. Why? Because if you cannot control what you are conscious of, the only thing you *can* be conscious of is that which is already around you. Therefore, what is, continues to be. You are *choosing* to be a product of your environment because you are *choosing* to allow your consciousness to settle and focus only on your environment. Your mind is basically only taking in what's being presented to it—what's around you. This is not real Thinking, it's being trained. It's no different than how animals are trained to do tricks at the circus. If animals could really Think, would a 15,000-pound elephant perform tricks all day for a handful of peanuts? Of course not. Would a killer whale jump through hoops at SeaWorld for a handful of fish? No way. These physically powerful animals are easily trained. They cannot choose a consciousness outside of the consciousness their trainers present to them— a pittance of food and very limited space in exchange for jumping through hoops. They lack the willpower to Think, which would switch their consciousness to the abundance of food and space to roam enjoyed by their free relatives living in the wild. What separates us from the animals is the fact that we can be presented with an idea and *choose* to Think something totally different! Wow! That is worth repeating. What separates us from the animals is the fact that we can be presented with an idea and *choose—by the power of our will—* to Think something totally different! Exercising this divine right places us at the table with the King of Kings as opposed to wallowing with the animals. But sadly—because we refuse to Think—many of us jump through hoops for a handful of peanuts and a fish every day.

When you understand how to control your consciousness by exercising your power of will, you will see that you can choose a different consciousness than what's around you. And you will notice that your environment will begin to change as a result. How else do you think a person like Jay-Z can go from Marcy Projects in Brooklyn to owning a share of the NBA's Brooklyn Nets and appearing on magazine covers such as *Forbes* and *GQ*? How else do you think a person like Freeway Ricky Ross, who was sentenced to life in prison with no possibility of parole (he was illiterate when he first went to prison), can re-emerge twenty years later as a free man, having read over 300 books and performing motivational speeches all across the country. *We must control our Thinking.*

The bottom line is that we must *make* our environment a product of our Thinking, not simply *allow* ourselves to become a product of our environment. So if you choose to be conscious only of what's already around you, then your environment will continue to be what's already around you. In other words, it will *appear* that you are a product of your environment.

Remember: no outside force has greater power over a person than the inner force of that person's Thinking.

You Cannot "Shut Off" Your Thinking

Picture a kitchen faucet with two knobs—one for hot water and one for cold water. Now picture turning on both knobs. There is hot water and cold water coming out of the spigot. Now imagine that—for whatever reason—you cannot turn off the water source. There will now always be water flowing from the spigot. You can only *adjust* the hot knob or cold knob to adjust the temperature of the water. You cannot ever stop the water from flowing. But you *can* control its temperature.

You will always be conscious of *something*. You cannot simply stop your consciousness. Even when you sleep, your brain and your heart are active and your subconscious is digesting what you were conscious of during your waking hours. In essence, you are akin to the water always flowing from the spigot. You cannot stop the flow, only control the temperature. Your willpower is the means that deliberately adjusts the hot water or cold water. You have the divine right to deliberately adjust and control your consciousness so that you are actually Thinking instead of simply being trained by what's around you. By choosing your Thinking, you place yourself in position to succeed!

Believe and Succeed

We've all heard the phrase "believe and succeed" many times. But its true significance and power requires some understanding. Once a belief takes hold in the subconscious mind (picture the mind becoming "magnetized" with the belief) the object of belief will appear. As a matter of fact, there is no way it can *not* appear. The will is the agency by which you control exactly what energy you allow to reach your mind.

When your senses initially perceive energy, you have only two options. You can accept the energy, or reject the energy. Here is where the will comes into play. In chapter 5, we showed that you must write out a precisely defined decision stating what you want. This precisely decided goal has energy. It is energy. Throughout the course of the day, your five senses constantly perceive energy. You see, hear, smell, touch, and taste many things. All of these things are energy. Your will must compare this received energy to the energy of your precisely defined goal. If the energy is the same, your will must allow the five senses to continue receiving the energy—accept it. Conversely, the will can—by shutting off the energy from the five senses and *replacing that energy with a new desired energy*—reject the unwanted energy. Remember that everything is energy.

The World Revolves Around *Me*

Let me tell you about the power of the will when it comes to manifesting a result through visualization and belief. Keep in mind that I wrote about this event just after it took place.

During the course of writing this book, I spent a considerable amount of time in Massachusetts. I'm not quite sure why, but there was a peaceful energy there, that I tapped into and that made the process of writing seem almost effortless at times. My preferred method of travel was by bus from New York. This method of travel was very efficient for me. Because I didn't have to drive, I could spend the four to five hour trip clearing my mind and writing.

Anyway, for one particular trip, I was planning to leave New York on the bus at 7 a.m. That morning, I went about my daily routine of awaking at 5 a.m., looking at my goal (which was a check written for a specific amount), and I played music that touched me emotionally and put me in a great mood. As I left my Wall Street office and entered the subway station on Broad Street, I felt powerful. As the J train approached, I felt great sayings come into my mind. I saw and felt myself as I was speaking on national television addressing the issues that seemed to be holding back lower-income communities. I was doing this in a way no one had ever done before, but in a way that was highly respected. I felt very powerful, as if I was the center of the world. (Ironically, a supervisor at a former job who was constantly reprimanding me once told me, "The world doesn't revolve around you.")

As I was leaving the subway station and walking toward the bus pickup area, I noticed that the line was particularly long for the 7 a.m. bus. Now, this was the first time I had caught this particular bus. As I walked into the station, there was a gentleman who had arrived just before me to present his ticket. Something—a feeling—said I should have been just a bit earlier, because I could tell by the line that had already formed outside, that the bus would be completely full. Anyway, as the gentleman before me was getting his ticket stamped, there was some talk by the people behind the counter that the bus was nearing capacity. They began to delay as they checked the number of people who had already lined up. They confirmed that the gentleman in front of me was okay to get on the bus. They stamped his ticket and he left the office to get in line for the bus.

As I stepped forward to the counter to pay, the attendant informed me that there didn't appear to be any more room on the 7 a.m. bus, and that I had to take the 8 a.m. bus. I told her "I want a ticket for the 7 a.m. bus," and that if there was no room, then I would take the 8 a.m. She took my money, gave me my change and my ticket. I rushed out of the office and got in line, directly behind the gentleman who had been in front of me in the office.

As the bus pulled up, and people started to board, I started telling myself, "I'm getting on *this* bus—the 7 a.m. bus. I'm going to be the last person to make it on the bus. This 7 a.m. bus will not leave without me!" *I actually told myself that.* As the seats started to fill up, the line slowed down. As there were about five people before me, three people were turned away; they were told to go back into the office. For what reasons, I am unsure.

Now, as the gentleman in front of me handed the bus attendant his ticket, there was again some confusion as they did a passenger count. And during the confusion, a girl who didn't even have a ticket got on the bus when the attendant wasn't watching. After the confusion, the attendant asked for the gentleman's ticket. He had already given the ticket to her, but she couldn't remember because she had been doing ten different things at once and handling a stack of tickets. And because she couldn't remember him giving her his ticket, she didn't want to let him on the bus. The gentleman explained that he had already given her his ticket, but she didn't want to listen to him. "Go back into the office. Get a ticket," she told him.

Now, during all this confusion, I had been so calm, as I just *knew* I was getting on that bus. And as a result of my calmness, I saw that the gentleman had already given the attendant his ticket. Now, she was about to make him get out of line and get another ticket. And of course, because I was next, I would get on the 7 a.m. bus instead of him. I'd be the last passenger. *But,* I calmly explained to the attendant that the gentleman in front of me had already given her his ticket and he was supposed to be on the bus. For some reason, she believed me and let him on the bus.

Then she said, "One more." I smiled, as I knew that was me. As I handed her my ticket, she looked at it and said, "No, eight o'clock." "What?" I said. I looked at the ticket as she handed it back to me. The ticket was written for 8 a.m., *not 7 a.m. as I had requested.* In my haste to get in line, *I had not checked the departure time on my ticket.*

I was immediately frustrated, and I went back to the office. I knew that there were many people behind me who were waiting to get on the bus. I started to pull out my laptop to work until the 8 a.m. bus came. I actually glanced up and watched TV for about a minute. Then for some reason, I went to counter and said, "Excuse me Miss. I asked for a 7 a.m. ticket. You gave me an 8 a.m. ticket even though there is room on the 7 a.m. bus. Part of me (my conscious reasoning) was saying this to get it off my chest, because I figured the bus had certainly been filled by now. But for some reason, when I spoke, the words came out "*is* more room on the 7 a.m. bus" instead of "*was* more room on the 7 a.m. bus." At the same moment I heard a faint "One more" through the walkie-talkie she was holding. She turned to me, and said, "One more. You go to the bus now." I ran out of the office, and there was almost a path for me, cutting through everyone else waiting, and the attendant guided me on the bus. I got on, but I did not see any available seat. Then my eyes found the empty seat. And the bus took off. I was the last person to make it onto the 7 a.m. bus, just as I had told myself. The 7 a.m. bus could not leave without me. And I thought to myself with a mischievous smile, "Maybe the world *does* revolve around me."

Ok, what's my point? "Big deal," you might say. "So you got on the 7 a.m. bus instead of the 8 a.m. bus. You got to Massachusetts an hour earlier."

The benefit was not so much in the hour that I gained (because I could have been productive waiting for the 8 a.m. bus since I had my laptop and iPhone with me), but rather the benefit was my understanding that I could have what I wanted if only I could *believe* it was mine by consciously picturing it and not accepting any alternative. A feeling of true belief—for whatever reason—is a powerful force that sweeps aside all obstacles.

Why did it mean so much for me to make the 7 a.m. bus? *Because I said that I was going to be on the 7 a.m. bus. And I had a definite reason for being on that bus.* In other words, getting on the 7 a.m. bus meant something to me. The "what" or Thought of "getting on the 7 a.m. bus" generated by my brain, was being driven by my Emotion generated by my heart.

Here is the most amazing fact ever discovered: there is only *one* thing in this universe that you have 100 percent control over—your Thinking.

Let that sink in, because with that one thing, you really do control *everything.* The world does revolve round me. And the great thing is, *the world revolves around you, too.* With your Thinking, you control everything.

Becoming a Money Magnet— Getting Hooked On Your Passion

> Money was never a big motivation for me, except as a way
> to keep score. The real excitement is playing the game.
> **—Donald J. Trump**

The number one form of energy that people want to draw into their lives using the Law of Attraction is the energy of *money*.

Make no mistake about it; money is definitely a potent form of energy. It's so potent that it can be thought of as a drug. As a matter of fact, it's a drug that's so powerful that even a very small amount of it can keep millions of people hooked on jobs they can't stand—just to get a little bit of money. A small, yet steady paycheck serves as a source of comfort and dependency for millions of people who have not yet learned the art of becoming a money magnet.

So what is a *money magnet?* Money magnets are people who

have the ability to attract money *directly to themselves from the source because they do what they love.*

One of the toughest hurdles for young entrepreneurs and business owners is the hurdle of attracting the money necessary to make their new (and unproven) enterprises profitable. Those who "make-it" do so because of their passion. The process of becoming a money magnet involves "quitting your day job," because the money you receive from a job is not attracted directly to you. It is attracted to the company (by the work you do), and then given to you in the form of a salary or wage. However, big money—the type you attract as a money magnet—is attracted *directly to you.* Think of cutting out the middleman. Furthermore, most people do not have passion for their job. If pressed for an honest answer, they would quit if they didn't need the paycheck.

Money from the source loves movement and speed. And what is ironic is that magnets in the physical world—the magnets that attract metal—are created by the movement of electrons. No movement of electrons means no magnet is created. And what I've found is that the speed of money is measured in MPH—Money, People, Hustle.

Money—Money is attracted to more money. Most entrepreneurs are short on cash in the beginning stages of their enterprises. I know we all want to build multimillion dollar businesses, but the key in the beginning is profitability. By creating and implementing a workable business plan and business case that creates product or provides service at a *profit*—even on a small scale—you can reinvest in yourself and your product and service. You will use a little money to begin drawing more money to you. As you become more consistent in this practice of reinvesting in yourself, you'll notice money coming to you at a faster rate.

People—This is an alliance of like-minded individuals rallying around a deeply rooted mission that breeds passion. If you're short on money, you must begin to develop a following of people who rally around a mission. Even if you do have money, a following of people is crucial to keeping and growing that money. I'm not a big fan of the word "networking." To me networking implies going to social events, handing out business cards, and trying to meet as many people as possible because "It's not what you know, it's who you know." Well, I think about that phrase a bit differently. I think it's really about *who knows you.* In other words, instead of trying to go out and meet everybody, work on becoming the person that everybody wants to meet. I prefer the term "alliance" over network because alliance signifies more of a rally around a common goal or mission. If you're short on money, you need to define a mission that touches your heart. In other words, define your passion. People follow passion.

There are many social media sites out there that people can utilize to help build a following. However, the followings that stand out are the ones that are backed by a mission of passion.

Hustle—Sheer effort and determination will make you stand apart from the crowd, making you respected and visible to those with money. I'm not talking about busy-work hustle. I'm talking about hustle backed by a mission that breeds passion. There really is no substitute for a person who is willing to go hard all the time because he is passionate about what he is doing. A person who is always hustling and giving an all-out effort is respected by those around him, and will begin to make his own "good luck." If you've got passion, hustling will become second nature to you. A person who is strictly "formal education and college degrees" is no match for a real hustler. And a person who does have some formal education *and* the passion of a hustler is a rare breed who will dominate his industry.

Lunch with a Millionaire

How many millionaires can you call right now and have lunch with? Well, that all depends on who you are.

I wrote an article in *GET MONEY Magazine* titled "The 7 Laws of Money." The Second Law of Money states: *If You Don't Know Money, No Money.* The first part of this law states:

> This is also called "money consciousness." The only reason a healthy, free man would choose to work the majority of his life for a pittance of a salary is that he does not know he can do better. When I say "know," I mean he has never been truly exposed to great riches to an extent that he would settle for nothing less. The only way to truly *know* money is to consistently see money.

When we live life through our passion, we can become money conscious. *We become conscious of the opportunities to get money when we are not blinded by our fear of losing money.* Wealthy people understand this principle. It is the reason why people with money like to be around other people with money. If you've ever been in a room full of people with money, you'll notice the energy that exists. Personally, I've had lunches and dinners with several millionaires. And I've had these engagements with millionaires during the times when I really did not have the kind of money they had on their level. But what I did have was *hustle that was bred through a deep passion.*

So frankly, if you're broke right now, you will probably have a hard time setting up an appointment or meeting to talk directly to a billionaire like Bill Gates, Warren Buffet, or Donald Trump. But don't worry, because through MPH (especially hustle), you will start to become a money magnet, and you will begin to see opportunities unfold for you.

What you'll notice as you MPH is the simultaneous development of workable action plans, by which you can see money before you actually have money. Remember: *consciousness creates*. Human imagination is the workshop in which the plans to acquire money are formulated. These plans are as valid as the money itself.

My office is in the Trump Building on Wall Street in New York. Some people think it's expensive to maintain an office here. But the way I see it, the dollar amount I pay is worth every penny when I compare it to the greater benefit I get by being surrounded by money. This is especially true for me, since I did not grow up in an environment where I was accustomed to seeing money, especially money on the scale that exists on Wall Street. Now, every day I see money. I know money. And I'm beginning to understand money. So there's no way that I cannot get money. So that's what I named my company (GET MONEY, Inc.) and my magazine (*GET MONEY Magazine*).

Now, I didn't always work in the Trump Building. My first "office" was the living room in my apartment in the South Bronx. The key here is that I had to begin to magnetize my mind (while I was in the South Bronx) with the consciousness of Wall Street. This is a process that requires discipline and imagination. The consciousness I experience from looking out from the Trump Building is quite different from the consciousness I experience from looking out from my building in the South Bronx.

There is no shame in growing up or living in a rough neighborhood. However, the challenge is to rise above our circumstances, and replace the images of poverty and lack with images of wealth and abundance. All lack and poverty is simply a lack of understanding.

People can go through their entire lives unhappy because they don't understand that they are literally magnets. If you don't understand that you are a magnet, you are not aware that you are—and have always been—constantly creating and pulling in everything you are allowing your consciousness to settle on. Remember, your Thinking is done through your brain *and* your heart. When you don't know this, you can become magnetized by the few people who do understand. That's why the media is so powerful. By constantly repeating a message to the five senses (connected to the brain) of a human, the brain will become magnetized with that message. If this message is continually presented, not only will the brain become magnetized, but so will the heart (you will develop an emotional attachment). And as we showed in chapter 4, the magnetic fields generated by the heart are 5,000 times stronger than those generated by the brain.

That's the very reason people feel like they literally can't stop smoking. They have developed an emotional attachment (in their heart) to cigarettes. The same is true with alcoholics. They have developed an emotional attachment to alcohol. Personally, I don't smoke. But I can smoke a cigarette right now, and not care, and not have a desire for another puff. And I can go weeks or months without a drink. *But I can't go a day without writing.* I love to write. I have developed an emotional dependency on writing. The good news for all of us is that we can "fall in love" with anything we choose. Wouldn't it be great if we literally couldn't stop getting money? Well, there are people in the world who can't. Everywhere they turn, money is attracted to them. They are money magnets!

Most people do not become magnetized by their passion. They become magnetized with things that other people want for them—mostly products and services that cause them to spend their money (as opposed to reinvesting their money back in themselves, their products, and services). This is the great divide between the haves and the have-nots. The haves are sellers and the have-nots are buyers. In order to accumulate great wealth (or any wealth at all) you must be a seller. A seller is a capitalizer of ideas. Money is attracted to workable action plans and ideas. That's why people who start off with no money can get money. It does take money to make money. Plans and ideas are simply undeveloped cash. And just like anything that must be developed, time and persistence are necessary for growth. Persistence is consistent action over time that develops into faith and belief.

Once I understood the Law of Attraction, I realized that everything I really wanted in my life, going back to my earliest memories, I got! This allowed me to remain calm and at ease when circumstances appeared in my life that were not to my liking.

If you don't understand that you are a magnet, you will forever be upset and frustrated with life because you will feel that things are "happening *to* you" that you don't want. You will feel like a victim who has no control of his life.

When you understand that you are a living magnet, you can be peaceful and calm—even in the midst of what may seem to be a disaster. You know that a bad situation is a result of your prior Thinking, and as such, you can repel and change that situation just the same as you attracted it—by your Thinking. How do you repel it? *Replace* the Thinking of the thing you don't want with the Thinking of what you *do* want.

The Rich Get Richer, the Poor Get Poorer: Is it True?

Lack of money tends to put people in bad moods. A bad mood means negative Emotion, which means less money.

Having money tends to put people in good moods. A good mood means positive Emotion, which means more money.

When you live in a poor urban neighborhood, or "the hood," one of the toughest aspects of "making it out" is to gain the ability to continuously hold the mental images of success against a "reality" which constantly screams otherwise. A person who lives surrounded by poverty or under not-so-ideal circumstances must develop a tremendously strong will in order to shut out the constant images of lack that he or she sees in the community on a constant basis. All around are signs and symbols that the reality of the world is one of failure. Even though the truth is that the world is overwhelmingly abundant, grasping this truth of abundance is very difficult if all you see around you says otherwise.

A person who already lives a life surrounded by wealth and abundance does not have to contend with creating a reality which is opposite of what they are presented with.

However in both cases, *gratitude* is the key to either attaining wealth or holding it. A feeling of gratitude is a powerful emotion that will switch you from a negative state of seeing poverty around you to a positive state of counting your abundant blessings. The first blessing to count is the awareness of the *ability* to change your environment—even though that change requires effort.

A rich man must continue to count his blessings and project the feeling of gratitude as he works in the field of his choice. Otherwise he will find his money leaving as fast as it came.

CHAPTER 8

Action—
The First Cause
of Emotion

Everything comes to him that hustles while he waits.
—Thomas A. Edison

If Thinking is intelligently directed and controlled human consciousness, *how* do we intelligently direct and control our consciousness? One word: action.

The purpose of this chapter is to change the cause and effect relationship we have with Emotions and actions. Most people's relationship looks like this:

Emotion / Cause
Action / Effect

In other words, they simply go through life acting like they feel. Many people get "stuck" in life because they *feel* a certain negative Emotion that they can't seem to shake. As a result, they continue to act according to how they feel—negatively.

This causes more negative Emotion. It's easy to see how people become depressed once they become trapped in a cycle they cannot seem to get rid of. When we feel a certain negative Emotion, even simple actions—like getting out of bed in the morning—can become difficult.

The problem lies in the fact that most people believe they are relegated to *act how they feel.* They believe that if—for whatever reason—they feel sad, they are supposed to act sad. They feel that if—for whatever reason—they feel angry, they are supposed to act angry. And they justify their actions because after all, they're just "acting how they really feel." But going back to our definition of Thinking, we can see that this type of behavior is not Thinking, but reacting. There is no benefit to prolonged acting out on negative Emotion. If anything, a negative Emotion is a signal that you should *do* something positive, ideally take action toward your predefined goal. Therefore, the moment you feel a negative Emotion, you have the right and duty to eliminate that negative Emotion as soon as possible—by taking action in the positive direction. Forming this habit gives you tremendous power because you have now changed the cause and effect relationship to the following:

Action / Cause
Emotion / Effect

Emotions follow action. Action is the means by which the Emotions are controlled. I don't care how down you are feeling. If you begin to act in a positive way, you will begin to feel positive. Remember, you are in 100 percent control. Thinking is intelligently directed and controlled consciousness. There is no way possible for you to Think, unless you can control your Emotions. It is for this purpose that we were given physical bodies.

Again, here is another reason to write out your goals and plans, and keep them in front of you (within your conscious) at all times. *See* your precision of decision. *Hear* your precision of decision. *Taste* your precision of decision. *Smell* your precision of decision. *Feel* your precision of decision. These are all physical actions you take to control your Emotion. You are in the process of shutting off the flow of negative Emotion from your heart. If you are actively working toward the attainment of a precisely defined and inspiring goal, there is no room in your consciousness for the negative. The beautiful thing about consciousness is that it limits us, in a good way; it focuses us. Because our consciousness is limited, we cannot feel a negative Emotion at the same time as we feel a positive Emotion. If you are actively engaged in doing what you love to do, your consciousness is on that, and that alone. The negative disappears because the negative cannot exist while the conscious is on the positive. The faith you feel as you actively work overshadows any fear that may have previously existed.

I believe one of the simplest, yet most important, things you can do to control your Emotion and put yourself in a great mood is to wake up early in the morning. To me early is 5 a.m. If you get into this habit—if you begin to *do* this—you will notice that you *feel* as if you are ahead of the game. And if you start to drag a bit in the late morning or early afternoon (because you got up so early), then *go* to the gym and work out. You'll notice a big difference once you get your body physically moving. To me, these are two simple, yet powerful things anyone can do to "feel good." You are controlling your Emotion.

We keep talking about controlling the Emotion, but here is a good place to reiterate exactly *why* this is so important. Your Thought and Emotion are the only things that you have absolute and complete control over. Your destiny is in your hands because of your right to control your Thought and Emotion. If you can form the habit of controlling these two things, you will be in position to benefit from the overflowing and bountiful rewards of life.

Okay. Let's get back to the topic of controlling your Emotion through action.

Many people lie in bed and oversleep because they don't *feel* like getting up. Many people don't go to the gym because they don't *feel* like going. Can you see how this reactionary behavior renders them helpless? Remember: the action is the cause. The feeling is the effect. And here is where our understanding of the science behind the Law of Attraction is so useful. Because we are now looking at the Law of Attraction as a science, we know that *the only way to benefit from the Law of Attraction is to maintain the positive Emotion.*

A major stumbling block of those who try to employ the Law of Attraction to work for them is their tendency to separate thinking from action. The common, but incorrect line of thought is as follows:

"So if I can attract the things and circumstances I want in my life just by thinking about them, I can sit down, think about what I want, and those things will magically come to me."

Eliminating this inaccuracy again requires us to understand what Thinking truly means. Thinking is intelligently directed and controlled consciousness, consisting of Thought and Emotion. Because actions control Emotion, you cannot get the most efficient use of your Thinking unless you are also *acting.* Most people view thinking as separate from action. They tend to think in one place and act in another. However, this should not be the case.

In other words, true Thinking is rooted in taking action, because it is the action—the doing—that controls the Emotion. And Emotion is part of Thinking.

Your Dreams Already "Are"

Electricity has *always* been there. *We just weren't plugged in.* Thomas Edison probably knew this.

When you understand that everything you can ever want or desire is *already* there, just waiting to be brought into useful form by your *consciousness*, taking action also becomes easier.

If you *knew* that there was one billion dollars-worth of gold buried twenty steps directly outside your back door, 100 feet below the earth in your back yard, how long do you think you would spend digging? You would spend most all of your waking hours digging. Furthermore, you would *find a way* to gain *more* waking hours. You would sleep less, eat less, ignore phone calls—nothing would matter except digging. Well, it's the same concept when it comes to anything you want in life. Remember from chapter 2, everything is energy. Therefore, whatever you want is already there. *It's all made of the same stuff.*

The simple difference between people who are doers and those who are not, is faith.

A non-doer thinks: *What if I dig, and there's nothing there?*

A doer thinks: *It's there, I just have to dig!*

Another major stumbling block along the road to achievement is the belief that the work you put in—the digging—is what creates your dreams and desires. This is not the case. It is the *feeling* from doing the digging that creates. This simple misguided thinking process eventually wears down even the most motivated people, because over time they begin to lose focus if they are engaged in work that does not evoke the positive Emotion. This explains the large number of hard working people who have little to show for their efforts.

You do not create what you want simply by hard work. As far as physical action is concerned, many animals are much stronger than man. To illustrate this, let's visit the farm for a minute. On the farm, the farmer will use strong animals such as horses and bulls to do the work and take action. These animals can outwork a human all day long. However, their only reward is a bit of hay and some grain. It is man who is the benefactor. *The true power is in the Thinking.* Man has nowhere near the physical strength of many animals, yet man is the master of beast because man has the ability to control his Emotion through action.

Internalize the truth that what you desire has *already* been created by your Thinking, and that actions control the emotional part of Thinking. Do the thing in the spirit that it has already been created.

Actions Perceive Energy

Do something. Right now—anything. Pick up your phone and call a client. Lift your leg. Or simply continue reading this book.

In every physical action you take, you are simply perceiving (and thus receiving) the energy that exists in your environment. In other words, *the result of every action is perception of energy.* You now know that *everything* is energy. No matter what actions you take, no matter how complex those actions may seem, all you are doing is perceiving the energy that presently exists in your environment. You cannot act in the future. You cannot act in the past. You can only act now—and right now, your "actions" are your five senses perceiving energy. You will feel a certain way based on the energy you allow your senses to perceive. It's really that simple.

There are energies around you right now that you have no clue about. You are not conscious of those energies. Either you don't have the sense to perceive them, or they are vibrating at such a high or low frequency—a frequency that is outside our perception range—that you cannot perceive it. If you blow a dog whistle, the dog will hear the whistle (perceive the sound energy) even though a person will hear nothing. A human's perception of sound energy is limited to energy vibrating between frequency ranges of 20–20,000 Hz. However, a dog can perceive sound energy vibrating between frequency ranges of 40–40,000 Hz. (Speaking of dogs, a dog's olfactory perception is the reason police use dogs to detect drugs. A dog's sense of smell is 100 times more acute than a human's sense of smell. Additionally, a great white shark can perceive a single drop of blood in an Olympic-sized swimming pool.)

You have a choice on whether or not to receive any energy. In other words, you have a choice in how you act. If you find yourself having negative thoughts about a person, keep your five senses away from them. Act in a different manner. Allow your senses to perceive a positive energy that will make you have positive Emotion. Our actions allow us to become conscious of—and thus "have"—the things and circumstances we desire.

You see, our bodies (through which we act) were given to us for the major purpose of servicing our minds. This is not to say that the body should be denied of satisfaction. As a matter of fact, the exact opposite is true. If the body is fundamentally used to serve the mind, the mind will be protected, free to generate the thoughts necessary to take care of the body. Furthermore, a person's major goal will almost inevitably be linked to some type of financial gain, which will satisfy the vast majority of the pleasures of the body. *At all times, the actions of our bodies should be such that our minds are perceiving the energy of our major goals.* Through our bodies' five senses (sight, touch, hearing, smell, taste), our bodies serve our minds.

We See What We Believe

The actions we take are the opportunities by which we form belief. By performing an action, no matter how complex, what you are really doing is using one of, or a combination of your five senses to perceive the energy around you. Over time, as you perceive energy, you will believe in that energy. Now, when you were born, you didn't know anything. But from the moment you were born, your senses have perceived the energy of your environment.

Belief is the deepest level of Thinking. It is the electromagnetic force that attracts. It is always "on," even when we are asleep. You are not really your physical body. You are an electromagnetic field, of which your physical body is the center. This electromagnetic "Thinking Field" has been largely ignored because it operates at such a high frequency that it is not detected. (The frequency would probably be higher than those of gamma rays on the electromagnetic radiation spectrum.) However, because this Thinking Field affects the physical environment (like invisible microwaves boil visible water), we can detect some the *effects* of this Thinking Field as it interacts with other fields and the environment. Our physical bodies are the instruments through which we both control this Thinking Field and detect the effects. We call these effects "the circumstances of life." It's what we get out of life. If you don't like what you are "seeing" (getting out of life), you must change what your physical body perceives, so that your Thinking Field changes. What are you allowing yourself to be conscious of? *A human being is a miraculous electromagnetic field that can both change itself and directly detect the effects that it causes! This is the Law of Attraction. No other form of energy has this ability!*

This seems ridiculously simple, so simple that it cannot possibly work. But if you are tired of receiving what you've been getting out of life, stop perceiving it. You cannot receive anything that you do not perceive. Take different actions to perceive different energy.

If you want a billion dollars, perceive the energy of a billion dollars through your actions. Write yourself a check for a billion dollars. Write out a billion dollar business plan. Tell yourself you are a billionaire. Stop hanging out with people who have poor mentalities. Read books by billionaires such as Bill Gates and Warren Buffet. Read the biographies of billionaires such as of Andrew Carnegie and John Rockefeller. Stop looking at your overdrawn bank account and write yourself a postdated check for the amount that you want. Sign it and feel its energy each and every day.

William James said, "We need only in cold blood *act* as if the thing in question were real, and it will become infallibly real by growing into such a connection with our life, that it will become real. It will become so knit with habit and emotion that our interest in it will be those which characterize belief."

Precisely-decided, written goals act as the anchors that constantly tell you exactly which energy to perceive through your actions. In the absence of goals, how do you know what actions to take to perceive energy? How do you know whether your actions perceive the desired energy? You don't.

What can you do *right now* to perceive the energy of your desire? The faster you move toward the thing you want, the faster it will move toward you!

Happiness is Found in Doing, Not Merely in Possessing

In the first issue of *Forbes* magazine (September 15, 1917), founder B. C. Forbes wrote, "Business was originated to produce happiness, not pile up riches." The great folly of life is this: people believe that happiness comes from the possession of things. As a result, they spend their lives chasing money and material possessions. They work jobs and do things they don't enjoy simply to get money. They believe that the things they buy with the money they get will somehow compensate for the unhappiness they experience from doing those things to get the money. This is not true. Happiness is found in doing, not merely in possessing.

This line of thinking is crucially important when defining goals. A car cannot make a person happy. A house cannot make a person happy. A spouse cannot make a person happy. Here is a major stumbling block of goal setting: *setting a goal on a material possession rather than a desired use of time.* People have this belief that if somehow they could only get a new house, a new car, or a new soul mate, then their life will be happy. But then they get it, and something is still missing. So they try yet a new house, new car, or new soul mate.

But let's not get confused. Material possessions are important. We need nice things in our lives. The key is to remember that these nice things in our lives are the effect of happiness (and the other positive Emotions), not the cause. In other words, the things or material possessions in your life should be a *reflection* of the happiness in your life, not the *reason* for your happiness.

Man's first duty is to gain a precision of decision on what makes him happy. Remember, it is the Emotion which drives a Thought into the subconscious mind, where the two mix with the power of Infinite Intelligence. There can be no success where positive Emotions are absent. Determine what it is that makes you happy, and begin immediately to do it.

"Work Is Play"

I know people who have spent years in college and graduate school because a certain career commands X amount of dollars in salary. They chose a career based on a salary or potential to make money. But they are miserable. So during the little amount of free time they have away from their career they spend their money on lots of things to compensate for their unhappiness. Additionally, they smoke or need lots of coffee and other stimulants to make it through the day. Most people never sit down and take time out to give serious consideration to what they actually enjoy doing.

We are not necessarily trying to get to a certain place in life; we are trying to get on a certain path. You are trying to get yourself into a position where you can do a certain thing—the thing you like to do. We all like to do certain things. Do them! Go ahead and do them. We all need money, but the aspect of getting money should not overshadow *how* you get it. It is the perception in society that a job with a salary does provide a certain amount of "security"; however this is not truly the case. The only type of security a person can have is to be great at providing a needed product or service. And that is determined by one person—you!

The most successful business owners understand that there are many things that need to be done in order to run a business, yet they do not do it all themselves. The struggle for beginning entrepreneurs and business owners is that there is so much that has to be done in order to operate a new business, and they end up doing it all themselves—either because they are afraid to "let go of their baby," or they do not have the means to compensate people for delegated tasks.

Successful businesses are those where owners operate within their circle of interest, and delegate everything else to others in their respected circles of interest. You want to create jobs with your business, not do everything yourself.

"I am the Master of my Universe!"

What are you doing right now? More than likely, what you are doing is dependent upon how you *feel*. But this is not the order we were designed to follow. Perhaps the toughest skill to master is the habit of acting to create an Emotion, as opposed to waiting on an Emotion before acting.

There is only one thing in this world that you have absolute control over, and that is your Thinking. And since your Thinking is comprised of the Thought of your brain, and the Emotion of your heart, you must learn how to control your Emotion. Action is the means by which we control your Emotion.

The most successful people in the world are the happiest people. This happiness is a result of always being in action—always doing. No matter how much money you acquire, when you just sit back and relax, you become frustrated. Why? The simple fact of the matter is that our physical bodies are tools designed for the purpose of controlling our Thinking—through action!

Unsuccessful people are always looking to sleep in on the weekends, take days off, take vacation time, and the like. Truly successful people don't want days off and vacations. And they surely don't want to sleep in. They truly enjoy what they are doing as they journey through life. Happiness comes from doing, not possessing. Personally, I feel that a person should sleep no more than six hours per night. For me, five hours is ideal. I've found that going to bed at midnight and awaking at 5 a.m. works best for me. I'll be a bit sleepy around 10 or 11 a.m., and that's when I go to the gym to get some more energy. Although time is a man-made concept, time waits for no man. Therefore, we must take full advantage of time by acting.

Here's a simple test to determine if you're doing the right thing. How do you feel? Since we have control over our Emotion, then if we are having a negative Emotion, then that means that there is something we are doing that is causing that Emotion. Change what you are doing, and your Emotion will follow suit. Most people go through life simply experiencing Emotions as they come and go. Then they act based on those Emotions. This is not how we were designed.

The *huge* misconception concerning the Law of Attraction is that you can simply conjure up positive thoughts in your mind and then sit back and wait for your fortune to magically be drawn to them, as if it were going to fall from the sky. The flawed nature of this thinking is that people don't understand the connection between action and Emotion. They don't understand what Thinking really means. Real Thinking is an active process. By definition, Thinking is the intelligently directed and controlled human consciousness. Part of Thinking is the Emotion. And action is the direct means to controlling the Emotion.

Humans are not designed to "feel good" without doing and taking action. Therefore, you cannot just "think positive thoughts" and "have positive emotions" and then sit back and not do anything and expect the Law of Attraction to benefit you. During the process of sitting back and not doing anything, your Emotion will not remain positive. Happiness comes from doing!

CHAPTER 9

The Genius Pyramid—
Sexed-Up Thinking

I just need someone to love.
—Lyric written by John Lennon and Paul McCartney

I have a secret to tell you. I didn't write *Electric Living* by myself.
Sure, the ideas flowed into my brain, and I sat down in front
on my laptop and wrote them out, but it kind of stands to reason that the writer of an inspirational book must be *inspired.*
And so I was. At times, writing *Electric Living* seemed effortless.

Genius sleeps within each one of us—a dormant potential energy that many individuals will never realize unless they
learn how to. Let's define "genius." *A genius is simply a person who consistently receives communication into their consciousness
directly from Infinite Intelligence.* Because Infinite Intelligence is
the source, the genius's work has that "something" that inher-
ently makes people take notice. It naturally makes people feel
good. When you are in the presence of genius, quite often
you are aware of it. We are often in awe of the thinking or
work of a genius because we can readily sense the presence of

a great and pure form of power being reflected through that person. The work of a genius bypasses the consciousness and touches you. It's that song, that poem, that piece of art, that speaker, that performance, that literary work, and so on, that leaves you impressed, and many times, simply "quieted." It's a gift to be touched by the thinking and work of someone who is so in tune with the higher vibrations of being. And here's the thing: most of us can have it—if only we decide to do the things that put us into the "zone" for it.

So how can individuals tap into and awaken their inner genius? We've already established that Thinking consists of two parts: the Thought from the brain, and the Emotion from the heart. Many times, in the often cold and calculating world of business, the finer emotions of great leaders are not given their due recognition by biographers and history books that chronicle their life journeys. As a matter of fact, throughout the pages of history, the men who became the world's great fortune builders—from John Rockefeller to Andrew Carnegie to Henry Ford—were chiefly inspired by the influence of the great loves in their lives. Many contend that their greatest motivator for reaching deeper within themselves to marshal these resources, came from the women they loved. The trigger of inspiration came from their ability to express the Emotions of love, sex, and romance—the three sides of the triangle in the Genius Pyramid.

The Genius Pyramid is the graphical representation we can use to illustrate how an individual's Thought of his or her *definite major purpose* in life (Genius Pyramid Base), when fueled and complemented by the Emotions of *love* (Genius Pyramid Side 1), *sex* (Genius Pyramid Side 2) and *romance* (Genius Pyramid Side 3) for a person (the right person), form a perfect pyramid through which the individual receives continuous

communication directly into his or her consciousness from
Infinite Intelligence.

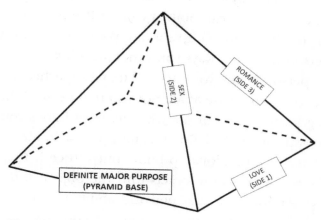

Figure 6. Genius Pyramid

Here's how this works: In the word *pyramid*, *pyra* means
"fire," the Universal Life Energy or cosmic force, and *mid*
stands for middle. So a pyramid harnesses cosmic energy and
preserves it. Pyramids attract energy and generate an energy
field which focuses the energy in the right direction.

For example, in the case where a man becomes attracted
to a woman, if his Thought is focused on his definite major
purpose in life (precision of decision) and is backed by the
Emotions of love, sex, and romance for that woman, he creates a continuous Thinking frequency of such a high vibration that his Thinking is continuously and emphatically
being received by Infinite Intelligence. Infinite Intelligence
is therefore continuously and emphatically responding. This
continuous communication coming directly from Infinite
Intelligence to a person's mind is known as "genius"—as I

defined earlier. A similar effect can be seen when a woman is attracted to a man.

It is important to note that individuals *must* have their base—their definite major goal or purpose in life. *That major goal or purpose cannot simply be the attainment of the object of their love.* Do not believe that you can build a Genius Pyramid by finding a person to fall in love with, working your charm and wooing that person in all the ways you can, and think it's enough to get that person to love you back. All that is superficial, and may not get you to first base at all, nor win that person's heart. So you've got three sides of the triangle, but where's your base? What is your precisely defined major purpose in life?

This is not a relationship book, but suffice it to say here that the way a person interacts with the object of their love has a *huge* impact on that person's ability to attain success. This is because the unique Thinking frequency mentioned earlier carries an energy that can lead to great accomplishment if channeled in the proper direction.

In a situation where love, sex, and romance are present and correctly aligned in equal measure and proportion to one another, an individual with a clearly defined purpose in life is virtually unstoppable!

Those who have felt the unique inspiration produced by the correct proportion of these Emotions yearn to keep it, because it gives them a distinct inspirational advantage in all that they do. Never is this more true than in their work—and it can move them from "work" to finding their "calling." As a matter of fact, the power of the synergy lifts that person out of the world of competition, and into the world of pure creativity. Now keep in mind that it is the *combination* of these three Emotions that lifts a person and gives them this advantage.

Take any one of the emotions away, and the Genius Pyramid lacks the full force of this effect. A person then falls from the level of creative genius to that of competitor. It is the presence of all three Emotions in balance that lifts individuals to genius—to the level where they are no longer competing with others; but rather, gauging their own selves as the measuring sticks for success. In short, they compete primarily with themselves. As far as relationships go, when individuals understand these three Emotions in another person, and tactfully cater to that understanding, they no longer have to worry about competition from others, since the understanding alone, allows them to rise above the competitive world into the creative world.

I will share something I saw one evening that sort of showcases this point. One night I was airing up my tires. It was cold, windy, and pouring cold rain. As I pulled up to the air machine, there was a car already there, and an older gentleman was kneeling down, struggling to put air in the tires of his car. He just couldn't seem to get the air hose to connect to the tire. As I got out of my car to help him, the passenger door of his car opened, and out stepped a small frail elderly lady who then opened an umbrella and held it over him.

Her presence changed him completely: as if not wanting her to see that he was struggling, suddenly, he wasn't. Gone was the frustration from his face, and as though he suddenly felt he could air these tires, and pronto, he proceeded to complete the job with a smile on his face and with strength and skill of someone half his age. He finished airing the tire, walked her back to the passenger side of the car, opened the door for her, then walked back to the driver's side and they left. Both had provided what the pyramid is about.

Consider yourself to be an engineer. Just as you cannot design a bridge without a solid foundation, you need to have your solid base to design your Genius Pyramid. Although the concept of the Genius Pyramid involves becoming inspired by another to the point of creative genius, we must remember that the purpose is to use that genius to perform the work in which you are involved. You are *not* to resemble some giddy teenager with a crush, daydreaming aimless thoughts with no accomplishment. On the contrary, your inspired genius is to be poured into your work with all the enthusiasm and passion you feel. Who do you have to inspire you to the mighty accomplishments and great Thinking level of genius?

Too often today, people are afraid to love another for fear of "putting themselves out there" or "getting their heart broken." Love is a gift, not an investment. It is to be given freely. When you truly love a person, your "reward"—if you will—is the feeling of inspiration you receive from the expression of that love. People guard their hearts under lock and key for fear of letting others in, and this also locks in the *expression* of love, that—if allowed to flow freely from their hearts—would create something tremendously inspiring.

Also, no one owes you anything when it comes to love. I know that's tough to swallow, but it's the truth. Remember, the only thing you have 100 percent control over is *your* Thinking—no one else's. Love comes and goes as it pleases, so enjoy it while it's there and become inspired to create something that *can* last forever, even if the person doesn't.

Energy is a beautiful thing. If you do truly love a person, and express that love *as a free gift*, it will be returned to you. It may not be returned by the person you express it to. Maybe it will. It may not be returned when you expect it. But it *will* be returned to you, just as you gave it—as a free gift.

CHAPTER 10

The Sixth Sense— Value Consciousness

There was always electricity . . . but it wasn't plugged in.
—Phyllis Diller

For all practical purposes, you are reading *Electric Living* because first, you know the Law of Attraction works, and understanding how it can work for you is of great value. We can all benefit: who doesn't want to live his or her life to the fullest, to nourish oneself in all ways, to attain a lifestyle of comfort and abundance? It's natural to want and have all these things. And, in most cases, to acquire all this is going to require money or its equivalent. The reality is that the most valuable things in life are the priceless and irreplaceable gifts that were already given to us *for free* at birth. They don't cost us anything. Our minds, souls, bodies, ambitions, dreams, and love cannot be replaced by any monetary value. They are ours for free. They cannot be bought with money. We cannot get them by reading a book. Recognition of these free irreplaceable gifts is key to acquiring all the other things—the replaceable things—that *do* cost money. Those things are not free.

Therefore, you are reading *Electric Living* to figure out how to get money because *you were already given for free all the things that money cannot buy.*

Throughout this book, I've repeated the phrase "consciousness creates." I've explained the laws of quantum physics to provide an understanding of the great Law of Attraction because what we call the "Law of Attraction" is simply the visible result of quantum physics in operation as we see it from the macroscopic level.

Since it is consciousness that creates, it only stands to reason that we must somehow become conscious of money and value in order to create money and value in our lives. So how do we become "money conscious"? How do we become conscious of money's energy so that we can "have" it in our lives, especially if we don't see money in the present physical environment we call reality? How do we become "value conscious"? How do we become conscious of the fact that a lasting friendship, a labor of love, a life of purpose, and the breath of life itself have a value that reach far beyond any monetary amount? Well, we have our eyes that can receive light energy. We have our ears that can receive sound energy. We have our senses of touch, taste, and smell which receive their respective energies as well. But how do we receive money and value energy if we do not receive it through one of our five physical senses?

The answer lies in our creative imagination, sometimes called the "sixth sense." We must develop our creative imagination so that we can perceive and become conscious of the pure money energy around us. I use the word *money* because it is tangible. But *value* is probably a better term. While not everyone has aspirations of becoming a multibillionaire, we all have aspirations of living a life of value. Individuals create their own value by means of their creative imagination.

The sixth sense is like the other five senses, in that we use it to become conscious by receiving a certain frequency range of energy. However, the sixth sense is different from the other senses because the energy of value is not perceived through any known or visible physical organ such as the eyes or ears.

Speaking of the physical senses, the visible spectrum is the part of the electromagnetic spectrum that is visible to the human eye. The typical human eye can respond to wavelengths from about 390 nanometers (violet) to roughly 750 nanometers (red). As wavelength decreases, frequency and energy increases.

So in terms of frequency, visible light corresponds to a band in the vicinity of 750–430 THz (THz = 10^{12} Hz). However, in general, detectable frequencies can range as high as 2.4×10^{23} Hz down to less than 1000 Hz. In other words, the human eye can only detect a tiny portion of the available electromagnetic spectrum. Using this available range of frequencies, our human eyes are conscious of only about 0.000001625 percent of these frequencies! The electromagnetic spectrum is ranges of energy.

If you look at the following graph—between infrared and ultraviolet—you will find the tiny sliver of energy we call visible light. All energy that is visible to the human eye falls within this 0.000001625 percent. There is so much energy out there that we are not conscious of. We cannot see gamma, X, ultraviolet, infrared, micro, or radio waves using our eyes alone. But it is these frequencies which make up the vast majority of the electromagnetic spectrum of energy. *And beyond the high frequency and energy levels of gamma rays would be found the frequency and energy levels of Thinking.*

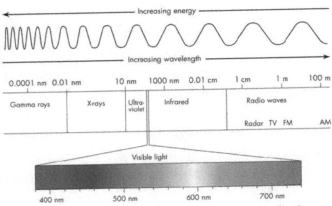

Figure 7. Spectrum of Electromagnetic Radiation

If you've ever seen any of the *Predator* movies, you'll recall that the Predator had a distinct advantage while hunting because he could actually "see" the infrared energy (or body heat) of his prey. In one particular scene of the original *Predator* movie, the character played by Arnold Schwarzenegger is right next to the Predator as it is hunting him. Since Arnold is covered in mud, his body heat is not visible, and the Predator passes right by him. Many of us are like this with money and the other valuable aspects of life. *Money and other intangible gems of value are right next to us, all around us in our environment, but we don't see them because we are lacking in the sense of creative imagination to become conscious of them. Consciousness creates.* If you are conscious of them, you can have them. If not, you simply miss out.

Ironically, value also has a wavelength and corresponding frequency. We detect this frequency through our creative imagination. If you've ever been suddenly inspired by a great and potentially profitable idea, this is your sixth sense "seeing" money. If you've ever felt the instinct to quickly help another person in a life or death situation, this is your sixth sense "seeing" value in life. We must exercise this sense; otherwise it loses its ability to function. Most of us are essentially blind to money and value. We fail to realize that all that we could ever want is already there, in our present environment. However, we usually lack the consciousness—or sense—to see it. Therefore, it is as if it did not exist.

Right now you are in the process of developing your sixth sense, so that you can become conscious of all the beautiful value already existing in your life. You want to see it all around you. This is done through the development of your creative imagination.

By nearly all accounts, John D. Rockefeller, Sr. was the wealthiest man in modern history. Rockefeller's net worth (adjusted for inflation in 2010 dollars) was estimated at $336 *billion* dollars. To give you an idea of how much money this really is, let's say that the average American family has a net worth of $100,000. If $100,000 is represented by a line that is only 1 millimeter long, then a line that represents Rockefeller's $336 billion would stretch for more than *2 miles*! I mention this example because when your consciousness is measuring value on a millimeter scale, money appears to be the most important thing in life. A few thousand dollars here or there can seem to have a significant value. But as millimeter consciousness stretches into meters, and then into hundreds of meters, and eventually miles, money begins to lose value to the individual. That is because value is a measure of *relative* worth, merit, or importance. Fifty thousand dollars appears to be a lot on the value scale of a person worth $100,000. But what is $50,000 to a billionaire? To a billionaire, $50,000 doesn't hold the same value. However, in each instance, there is no scale that can measure the value of life.

John Rockefeller lived to be ninety-seven years old. A year to him is the same as a one to you.

The true purpose of getting money is to fully experience the things in life that money cannot buy. Ironically, understanding that money has a limited value when compared to the important things in life is the key to becoming exceedingly wealthy.

More than pulling objects and circumstances to us, what we are doing is pushing our inner world—our Thinking—outward. Our outer world conforms to match. We will see only that which we are looking for. As our consciousness changes, so does our outer world appear to change based on that consciousness.

We tend to think of the Law of Attraction as magically pulling houses, cars, and money to us. However, what is actually taking place is those things are simply revealed to us. They've been there all along. We just didn't have the consciousness to see them in their present form. As our consciousness changes, our circumstances will change, just as changes in temperature will change ice to liquid and water to steam—*all of which are simply H_2O being revealed in different forms.* The key is that if we had no way to detect temperature and make the connection between temperature change and the different forms of H_2O, it would appear to be magic that ice could somehow change into the seemingly different liquid, which could then somehow change into the seemingly different steam. As a matter of fact, there was a time—during the infancy of science—that the changing forms of water did appear to be some type of magic. Today, the change is an easily understood concept taught in elementary school science books.

And so it will be with the Law of Attraction. In the near future, the science behind the Law of Attraction will be understood as easily as the science of changing the temperature of water to form ice or steam. Then we will all be living electrically. Remember, electricity has always been there. We just weren't plugged in.

Consciousness creates. We call it magic until we understand. But once we understand, we simply call it *science*.

About the Author

KOLIE CRUTCHER is the founder and CEO of the Wall Street publishing company, GET MONEY, Inc., (publisher of *GET MONEY Magazine*) located in the Trump Building in the heart of New York City's financial district. *GET MONEY Magazine* has become the premier lifestyle magazine for the young urban entrepreneur, and though still independent, has caught the attention of notables such as Ricky Ross, Russell Simmons, Snoop Dogg, and Steve Forbes.

Kolie is an alumnus of Mississippi State University, and has earned a bachelor of science degree in electrical engineering, with a minor in mathematics. Before founding GET MONEY, Inc., he worked as an engineer at major firms such as BellSouth Telecommunications, Florida Power & Light, and the Consolidated Edison Company of New York. His in-depth understanding of electrical engineering principles and practical engineering experience formed the basis of ideas expressed in *Electric Living*. *Electric Living* guides the reader through the step-by-step mental process of creating their own powerful life.

Through his unique experience as an engineer, writer, publisher, and business owner in New York City, Kolie Crutcher is able to reach the hearts of the urban community and the minds of corporate America. His writing and publishing has a scientific approach to success and wealth creation, while at the same captivates the younger generation with an unmistakable swagger.

He can be reached at:

www.thesciencebehindthelawofattraction.com

Other Books by
Bettie Youngs Book Publishers

The Law of Attraction for Teens
How to Get More of the Good Stuff, and Get Rid of the Bad Stuff!

Christopher Combates

Whether it's getting better grades, creating better relationships with your friends, parents, or teachers, or getting a date for the prom, the Law of Attraction just might help you bring it about. It works like this: Like attracts like. When we align our goals with our best intentions and highest purpose, when we focus on what we want, we are more likely to bring it about. This book will help you to:

- Understand when the Law of Attraction is working positively (producing the results you want)
- Use stress, pressure and anxiety to your advantage
- Learn positive techniques you can use for bringing about a better life; and,
- Learn how to think, act, and communicate in the positive way.

ISBN: 978-1-936332-29-8 • $14.95
ePub ISBN: 978-1-936332-30-4

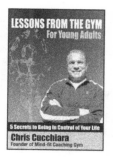

Lessons from the Gym for Young Adults
5 Secrets to Being in Control of Your Life

Chris Cucchiara

Do you lack self-confidence or have a difficult time making decisions? Do you ever have a tough time feeling a sense of purpose and belonging? Do you worry that you don't measure up? Or that you're doing what other people want of you, instead of what you want?

Growing up, Chris Cucchiara felt the same, until he joined a gym. The lessons he learned helped him gain the confidence he needed to set and achieve goals. In *Lessons from the Gym for Young Adults*, Chris shares his experiences and powerful insights and shows you how to:

- develop mental toughness (a life without fear, stress, and anger);
- develop an attitude to get and stay healthy and fit;
- build an "athlete for life" mentality that stresses leadership and excellence as a mindset; and,
- stay motivated, and set and achieve goals that matter.

ISBN: 978-1-936332-38-0 • $14.95
ePub ISBN: 978-1-936332-34-2

The Maybelline Story—And the Spirited Family Dynasty Behind It

Sharrie Williams

Throughout the twentieth century, Maybelline inflated, collapsed, endured, and thrived in tandem with the nation's upheavals. Williams, to avoid unwanted scrutiny of his private life, cloistered himself behind the gates of his Rudolph Valentino Villa and ran his empire from a distance. This never before told story celebrates the life of a man whose vision rocketed him to success along with the woman held in his orbit: his brother's wife, Evelyn Boecher—who became his lifelong fascination and muse. A fascinating and inspiring story, a tale both epic and intimate, alive with the clash, the hustle, the music, and dance of American enterprise.

A richly told story of a forty-year, white-hot love triangle that fans the flames of a major worldwide conglomerate. —**Neil Shulman, Associate Producer,** *Doc Hollywood*

Salacious! Engrossing! There are certain stories, so dramatic, so sordid, that they seem positively destined for film; this is one of them. —*New York Post*

ISBN: 978-0-9843081-1-8 • $18.95
ePub ISBN: 978-1-936332-17-5

Diary of a Beverly Hills Matchmaker

Marla Martenson

Marla takes her readers for a hilarious romp through her days in an exclusive matchmaking agency. From juggling the demands of out-of-touch clients and trying to meet the capricious demands of an insensitive boss to the ups and downs of her own marriage with a husband who doesn't think that she is "domestic" enough, Marla writes with charm and self-effacement about the universal struggles of finding the love of our lives—and knowing it.

Martenson's irresistible quick wit will have you rolling on the floor. —**Megan Castran, international YouTube Queen**

ISBN: 978-0-9843081-0-1 • $14.95
ePub ISBN: 978-1-936332-03-8

The Rebirth of Suzzan Blac

Suzzan Blac

A horrific upbringing and then abduction into the sex slave industry would all but kill Suzzan's spirit to live. But a happy marriage and two children brought love—and forty-two stunning paintings, art so raw that it initially frightened even the artist. "I hid the pieces for 15 years," says Suzzan, "but just as with the secrets in this book, I am slowing sneaking them out, one by one by one." Now a renowned artist, her work is exhibited world-wide.

A story of inspiration, truth and victory.

A solid memoir about a life reconstructed. Chilling, thrilling, and thought provoking. —**Pearry Teo, Producer,** *The Gene Generation*

ISBN: 978-1-936332-22-9 • $16.95
ePub ISBN: 978-1-936332-23-6

Blackbird Singing in the Dead of Night
What to Do When God Won't Answer

Gregory L. Hunt

Pastor Greg Hunt had devoted nearly thirty years to congregational ministry, helping people experience God and find their way in life. Then came his own crisis of faith and calling. While turning to God for guidance, he finds nothing. Neither his education nor his religious involvements could prepare him for the disorienting impact of the experience.

Alarmed, he tries an experiment. The result is startling—and changes his life entirely.

In this most beautiful memoir, Greg Hunt invites us into an unsettling time in his life, exposes the fault lines of his faith, and describes the path he walked into and out of the dark. Thanks to the trail markers he leaves along the way, he makes it easier for us to find our way, too. —**Susan M. Heim, co-author,** *Chicken Soup for the Soul, Devotional Stories for Women*

Compelling. If you have ever longed to hear God whispering a love song into your life, read this book. —**Gary Chapman,** *NY Times* **bestselling author,** *The Love Languages of God*

ISBN: 978-1-936332-07-6 • $15.95
ePub ISBN: 978-1-936332-18-2

DON CARINA
WWII Mafia Heroine

Ron Russell

A father's death in Southern Italy in the 1930s—a place where women who can read are considered unfit for marriage—thrusts seventeen-year-old Carina into servitude as a "black widow," a legal head of the household who cares for her twelve siblings. A scandal forces her into a marriage to Russo, the "Prince of Naples."

By cunning force, Carina seizes control of Russo's organization and disguising herself as a man, controls the most powerful of Mafia groups for nearly a decade. Discovery is inevitable: Interpol has been watching. Nevertheless, Carina survives to tell her children her stunning story of strength and survival.

ISBN: 978-0-9843081-9-4 • $15.95
ePub ISBN: 978-1-936332-49-6

Living with Multiple Personalities
The Christine Ducommun Story

Christine Ducommun

Christine Ducommun was a happily married wife and mother of two, when—after moving back into her childhood home—she began to experience panic attacks and a series of bizarre flashbacks. Eventually diagnosed with Dissociative Identity Disorder (DID), Christine's story details an extraordinary twelve-year ordeal unraveling the buried trauma of her past and the daunting path she must take to heal from it. Therapy helps to identify Christine's personalities and understand how each helped her cope with her childhood, but she'll need to understand their influence on her adult life.

Fully reawakened and present, the personalities compete for control of Christine's mind as she bravely struggles to maintain a stable home for her growing children. In the shadows, her life tailspins into unimaginable chaos—bouts of drinking and drug abuse, sexual escapades, theft and fraud—leaving her to believe she may very well be losing the battle for her sanity. Nearing the point of surrender, a breakthrough brings integration.

A brave story of identity, hope, healing and love.

Reminiscent of the Academy Award-winning *A Beautiful Mind*, this true story will have you on the edge of your seat. Spellbinding! —**Josh Miller, Producer**

ISBN: 978-0-9843081-5-6 • $16.95
ePub ISBN: 978-1-936332-11-3

Amazing Adventures of a Nobody
Leon Logothetis

Tired of his disconnected life and uninspiring job, Leon leaves it all behind—job, money, home even his cell phone—and hits the road with nothing but the clothes on his back. His journey from Times Square to the Hollywood sign relying on the kindness of strangers and the serendipity of the open road, inspires a dramatic and life changing transformation.

A gem of a book; endearing, engaging and inspiring. —**Catharine Hamm,** *Los Angeles Times* **Travel Editor**

Leon reaches out to every one of us who has ever thought about abandoning our routines and living a life of risk and adventure. His tales of learning to rely on other people are warm, funny, and entertaining. If you're looking to find meaning in this disconnected world of ours, this book contains many clues. —*Psychology Today*

ISBN: 978-0-9843081-3-2 • $14.95
ePub ISBN: 978-1-936332-51-9

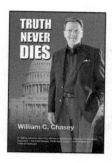

Truth Never Dies
William C. Chasey

A lobbyist for some 40 years, William C. Chasey represented some of the world's most prestigious business clients and twenty-three foreign governments before the US Congress. His integrity never questioned.

All that changed when Chasey was hired to forge communications between Libya and the US Congress. A trip he took with a US Congressman for discussions with then Libyan leader Muammar Qadhafi forever changed Chasey's life. Upon his return, his bank accounts were frozen, clients and friends had been advised not to take his calls.

Things got worse: the CIA, FBI, IRS, and the Federal Judiciary attempted to coerce him into using his unique Libyan access to participate in a CIA-sponsored assassination plot of the two Libyans indicted for the bombing of Pan Am flight 103. Chasey's refusal to cooperate resulted in the destruction of his reputation, a six-year FBI investigation and sting operation, financial ruin, criminal charges, and incarceration in federal prison.

A somber tale, a thrilling read. —**Gary Chafetz, author,** *The Perfect Villain: John McCain and the Demonization of Lobbyist Jack Abramoff*

ISBN: 978-1-936332-46-5 • $24.95
ePub ISBN: 978-1-936332-47-2

Out of the Transylvania Night

Aura Imbarus

A Pulitzer-Prize entry

"I'd grown up in the land of Transylvania, homeland to Dracula, Vlad the Impaler, and worse, dictator Nicolae Ceausescu," writes the author. "Under his rule, like vampires, we came to life after sundown, hiding our heirloom jewels and documents deep in the earth." Fleeing to the US to rebuild her life, she discovers a startling truth about straddling two cultures and striking a balance between one's dreams and the sacrifices that allow a sense of "home."

Aura's courage shows the degree to which we are all willing to live lives centered on freedom, hope, and an authentic sense of self. Truly a love story! —**Nadia Comaneci, Olympic Champion**

A stunning account of erasing a past, but not an identity. —**Todd Greenfield, 20th Century Fox**

ISBN: 978-0-9843081-2-5 • $14.95
ePub ISBN: 978-1-936332-20-5

On Toby's Terms

Charmaine Hammond

On Toby's Terms is an endearing story of a beguiling creature who teaches his owners that, despite their trying to teach him how to be the dog they want, he is the one to lay out the terms of being the dog he needs to be. This insight would change their lives forever.

Simply a beautiful book about life, love, and purpose. —**Jack Canfield, compiler,** *Chicken Soup for the Soul* **series**

In a perfect world, every dog would have a home and every home would have a dog like Toby! —**Nina Siemaszko, actress,** *The West Wing*

This is a captivating, heartwarming story and we are very excited about bringing it to film. —**Steve Hudis, Producer**

Soon to be a major motion picture!

ISBN: 978-0-9843081-4-9 • $15.95
ePub ISBN: 978-1-936332-15-1

The Morphine Dream

Don Brown with Boston Globe Pulitzer nominated Gary S. Chafetz

At 36, high-school dropout and a failed semi-professional ballplayer Donald Brown hit bottom when an industrial accident left him immobilized. But Brown had a dream while on a morphine drip after surgery: he imagined himself graduating from Harvard Law School (he was a classmate of Barack Omaba) and walking across America. Brown realizes both seemingly unreachable goals, and achieves national recognition as a legal crusader for minority homeowners. This intriguing tale of his long walk—both physical and metaphorical—is an amazing story of loss, gain and the power of perseverance.

"An incredibly inspirational memoir." **—Alan M. Dershowitz, professor, Harvard Law School**

ISBN: 978-1-936332-25-0 • $16.95
ePub ISBN: 978-1-936332-26-7

Hostage of Paradox: A Memoir

John Rixey Moore

A profound odyssey of a college graduate who enlists in the military to avoid being drafted, becomes a Green Beret Airborne Ranger, and is sent to Vietnam where he is plunged into high-risk, deep-penetration operations under contract to the CIA—work for which he was neither specifically trained nor psychologically prepared, yet for which he is ultimately highly decorated. Moore survives, but can't shake the feeling that some in the military didn't care if he did, or not. Ultimately he would have a 40-year career in television and film.

A compelling story told with extraordinary insight, disconcerting reality, and engaging humor. **—David Hadley, actor, *China Beach***

ISBN: 978-1-936332-37-3 • $24.95
ePub ISBN: 978-1-936332-33-5

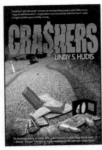

Crashers
A Tale of "Cappers" and "Hammers"
Lindy S. Hudis

The illegal business of fraudulent car accidents is a multi-million dollar racket, involving unscrupulous medical providers, personal injury attorneys, and the cooperating passengers involved in the accidents. Innocent people are often swept into it.

Newly engaged Nathan and Shari, who are swimming in mounting debt, were easy prey: seduced by an offer from a stranger to move from hard times to good times in no time, Shari finds herself the "victim" in a staged auto accident. Shari gets her payday, but breaking free of this dark underworld will take nothing short of a miracle.

A riveting story of love, life—and limits. A non-stop thrill ride. **—Dennis "Danger" Madalone, stunt coordinator for the television series,** *Castle*

ISBN: 978-1-936332-27-4 • $16.95
ePub ISBN: 978-1-936332-28-1

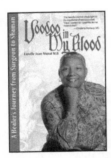

Voodoo in My Blood
A Healer's Journey from Surgeon to Shaman
Carolle Jean-Murat, M.D.

Born and raised in Haiti to a family of healers, US trained physician Carolle Jean-Murat came to be regarded as a world-class surgeon. But her success harbored a secret: in the operating room, she could quickly intuit the root cause of her patient's illness, often times knowing she could help the patient without having to put her under the knife. Carolle knew that to fellow surgeons, her intuition was best left unmentioned. But when the devastating earthquake hit Haiti and Carolle returned to help—she had to acknowledge the shaman she had become.

This mesmerizing story takes us inside the secret world of voodoo as a healing practice, and sheds light on why it remains a mystery to most and shunned by many.

"A beautiful memoir." **—Christiane Northrup, M.D.**

"A masterpiece! Truly enlightening. A personal story you won't soon forget." **—Adrianne Belafonte-Bizemeyer**

ISBN: 978-1-936332-05-2 • $24.95
ePub ISBN: 978-1-936332-04-5

Universal Co-opetition
Nature's Fusion of
Co-operation and Competition

V Frank Asaro

A key ingredient in business success is competition—and cooperation. Too much of one or the other can erode personal and organizational goals. This book identifies and explains the natural, fundamental law that unifies the apparently opposing forces of cooperation and competition. By finding this synthesis point in a variety of situations—from the personal to the organizational—this is the ultimate recipe for individual or group success.

"Your extraordinary book has given me valuable insights." —**Spencer Johnson, author,** *Who Moved My Cheese*

ISBN: 978-1-936332-08-3 • $15.95
ePub ISBN: 978-1-936332-09-0

It Started with Dracula
The Count, My Mother, and Me

Jane Congdon

The terrifying legend of Count Dracula silently skulking through the Transylvania night may have terrified generations of filmgoers, but the tall, elegant vampire captivated and electrified a young Jane Congdon, igniting a dream to one day see his mysterious land of ancient castles and misty hollows. Four decades later she finally takes her long-awaited trip—never dreaming that it would unearth decades-buried memories, and trigger a life-changing inner journey. A memoir full of surprises, Jane's story is one of hope, love—and second chances.

Unfinished business can surface when we least expect it. *It Started with Dracula* is the inspiring story of two parallel journeys: one a carefully planned vacation and the other an astonishing and unexpected detour in healing a wounded heart. —**Charles Whitfield, MD, bestselling author of** *Healing the Child Within*

An elegantly written and cleverly told story. An electrifying read. —**Diane Bruno, CISION Media**

ISBN: 978-1-936332-10-6 • $15.95
ePub ISBN: 978-1-936332-11-3

Bettie Youngs Books

We specialize in MEMOIRS
. . . books that celebrate
fascinating people and
remarkable journeys

In bookstores everywhere, online, Espresso,
or from the publisher, Bettie Youngs Books.

VISIT OUR WEBSITE AT
www.BettieYoungsBooks.com

To contact:
info@BettieYoungsBooks.com

CPSIA information can be obtained
at www.ICGtesting.com
Printed in the USA
FSHW021656220520
70364FS